I Never Knew That
About
YORKSHIRE

CHRISTOPHER WINN

I Never Knew That
About
YORKSHIRE

ILLUSTRATIONS BY
Mai Osawa

EBURY
PRESS

3 5 7 9 10 8 6 4 2

Published in 2010 by Ebury Press, an imprint of Ebury Publishing

A Random House Group Company

Text © Christopher Winn 2010
Illustrations © Mai Osawa 2010

The Random House Group Limited Reg. No. 954009

Addresses for companies within the Random House Group can be found at
www.randomhouse.co.uk

A CIP catalogue record for this book is available from the British Library

The Random House Group Limited supports The Forest Stewardship
Council (FSC), the leading international forest certification organisation. All our titles
that are printed on Greenpeace approved FSC certified paper carry the FSC logo. Our
paper procurement policy can be found at www.rbooks.co.uk/environment

Mixed Sources
Product group from well-managed
forests and other controlled sources
www.fsc.org Cert no. TT-COC-2139
FSC © 1996 Forest Stewardship Council

To buy books by your favourite authors and register for offers visit
www.rbooks.co.uk

Series designed by Peter Ward

Typeset by Palimpsest Book Production Limited,
Grangemouth, Stirlingshire
Printed and bound in Great Britain by
CPI Mackays, Chatham, ME5 8TD

ISBN: 978 0 09 193313 5

For Stephen and Carolyn,
with all our thanks for your generous
hospitality and kindness

Contents

PREFACE

Yorkshire, 'God's Own County', is big in every way. It is the biggest county in Britain, with more acres than there are letters in the Bible. The West Riding alone is bigger than any county in England.

Yorkshire has England's biggest vale, biggest medieval cathedral, biggest abbey ruins, biggest parish church, the world's biggest fish and chip shop and Britain's tallest man.

Yorkshire is not just big but beautiful too, an unmatched array of breathtaking scenery, with wide skies, undulating wolds and shifting shores in the east; high moors, quaint fishing villages and spectacular cliffs in the north; deep, narrow, populous valleys and empty, spectacular limestone dales in the west.

York was the Roman capital of the North, chief town to the Vikings, has Europe's best medieval streets and England's longest city walls. The Saxon town of Ripon is Britain's oldest city. The Norman walls of Richmond are Britain's oldest castle walls, the keep at Conisbrough England's oldest round keep.

York is the ecclesiastical capital of the North. The first Christian Roman Emperor, Constantine, was proclaimed in York. The English Roman church was born in Whitby. Yorkshire has not one but two of England's great medieval cathedrals, and a clutch of England's most beautiful churches.

Yorkshire has architectural treasures, palaces like Castle Howard and Harewood, stately homes such as Wentworth Woodhouse, Nostell Priory and Burton Agnes.

Yorkshire can boast of England's first seaside resort, first industrial model village, first railway museum, and was the first place in the world to appear on film.

Yorkshire was the powerhouse of the Industrial Revolution, had the biggest mills in the world and was the world's biggest producer of iron and steel. Yorkshire natives invented the aeroplane, stainless steel, Portland cement, the hydraulic press, cat's eyes and the tea shop.

Yorkshire is the home of the Brontës, J.B. Priestley, Alan Bennett, Philip Larkin, Tristram Shandy, Dracula, James Herriot. And in sport, Yorkshire is the birthplace of Rugby League and home to the oldest classic horse race and the oldest football club in the world.

Truly, Yorkshire is a kingdom unto itself.

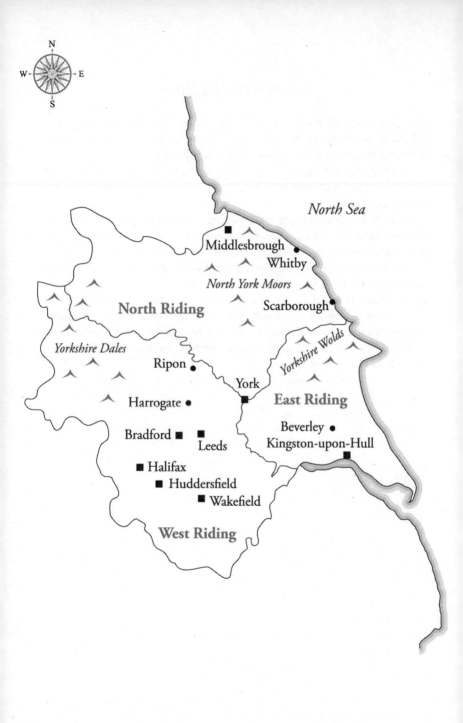

Yorkshire's Ridings

Since virtually all the stories in *I Never Knew That About Yorkshire* were played out in the context of the three historic Yorkshire Ridings – East, West and North – I have arranged this book by Ridings.

The Ridings, or 'Thridings', are of Viking origin, from the term Threthingr or a 'third part', and have been inextricably wound up with the history of Yorkshire for over 1,000 years.

Each Riding is distinctive in its history, topography, feel and character. They are divided by natural boundaries, East and North by the River Derwent, West and North by the River Ouse and its tributaries the Ure and Nidd.

The East Riding is farming country and has the Wolds, gentle and rolling, the mighty Humber, the low, shifting coastline and glorious churches. The North Riding shares the Dales with the West, and has the wild North York Moors, steep fishing towns and seaside resorts. The West Riding has the Dales, an industrial heritage second to none, magnificent architecture, and the Brontës.

Yorkshire's two ancient cathedral cities of York and Ripon I have brought together in the same chapter.

York and Ripon

York and Ripon

York Minster, largest medieval Gothic cathedral in northern Europe

York

*'The History of York is the
History of England'*
GEORGE VI

YORK is one of the oldest and most attractive of English cities, nestling at the heart of THE LARGEST ENGLISH VALE, THE VALE OF YORK, and is the capital and crowning glory of THE LARGEST ENGLISH COUNTY, YORKSHIRE.

There are wonderful walks along York's 3 miles (5 km) of ancient walls, which almost completely encircle the old city, enclosing some 263 acres (106 ha), and are pierced by many battlemented gates – including WALMGATE,

THE LAST CITY GATE IN ENGLAND TO RETAIN ITS BARBICAN.

York sits at the head of the broad valley between the Yorkshire Dales and the North York Moors, where the River Fosse joins the River Ouse, and at the lowest point where the Ouse is bridgeable – and has been recognised as an important strategic site since prehistoric times.

Eboracum

Modern York evolved from the Roman fort of EBORACUM, which was established on the Ouse in AD 71, and quickly became the most important settlement in the north of Roman Britain. The Emperor SEPTIMUS SEVERUS ruled the entire Roman Empire from Eboracum for two years, before he died there in AD 211, and is buried somewhere beneath the old city. In AD 306 the Emperor CONSTANTIUS CHLORUS died in Eboracum, and his son, CONSTANTINE THE GREAT, was proclaimed Emperor there. The most substantial relic left over from the Roman city is the MULTANGULAR TOWER in Museum Gardens, which was built in 209 while the Emperor Severus was in residence, and was part of the Roman wall overlooking the Ouse.

Eferwic

In the 7th century the settlement became the capital of the Saxon King Edwin of Northumbria, and was known as EFERWIC. A small wooden church was built on the site of the Roman fortress and here, in 627, Edwin was baptised by THE FIRST BISHOP OF YORK, PAULINUS. The well from which the water came for the baptism can still be seen in the crypt of the present minster.

Paulinus also founded ST PETER'S SCHOOL in that same year – making St Peter's THE THIRD OLDEST SCHOOL IN THE WESTERN WORLD. York was raised to an archbishopric in 735 and became the ecclesiastical capital of the North. In 2005 JOHN SENTAMU was enthroned as Archbishop of York – and as THE ANGLICAN CHURCH'S FIRST BLACK ARCHBISHOP.

Jorvik

In 867 Eferwic was captured by the Vikings and for the next 100 years was known as JORVIK, part of the Danelaw. Very little was thought to have survived of Jorvik, except the name York and the frequent use of 'gate', the Norse word for street, in many of the modern road names. However, in 1973, during excavations in Coppergate, three timber buildings and some furniture from the Viking period were discovered, so well preserved in wet peat that they could be reassembled for a new museum. The JORVIK VIKING CENTRE, in Coppergate, is now one of York's most popular tourist attractions.

Jorvik was THE LAST TOWN TO BE FREED FROM VIKING RULE before England became united under the Anglo-Saxons in 965. A survivor from that second Saxon occupation is the tower of ST MARY'S BISHOPHILL JUNIOR, THE OLDEST EXAMPLE OF ECCLESIASTICAL ARCHITECTURE IN YORK. It dates from the 10th century and includes Roman brickwork.

Norman York

After the Norman Conquest, William the Conqueror came to York to crush dissent in the North, and after burning the town down, he rebuilt it with two castles to guard the Ouse, extended the walls to their present position, and gave the go-ahead for a huge new minster to replace the Saxon one that had been burned down.

CLIFFORD'S TOWER, named after Roger de Clifford who was hanged

there after the battle of Boroughbridge in 1322, now stands on the mound of the principal Norman castle. Built in 1244, it is THE ONLY QUATRE-FOIL PLAN CASTLE IN ENGLAND, the design being based on the Château d'Etampes near Paris. The rest of the castle buildings now make up the Castle Museum and contain the condemned cell where the highwayman DICK TURPIN spent his last night in 1739 before going to the gallows. He is buried not far away in St George's churchyard.

William II founded ST MARY'S ABBEY in York in 1089. Only ruins remain of the abbey church, but the 15th-century Abbot's Lodging, called the King's Manor, is now part of York University.

The Norman city walls were rebuilt in the 13th century and the walls we walk on today date from this time. They are THE LONGEST CITY WALLS IN ENGLAND. Work also started in the 13th century to transform the Norman minster.

York Minster

By the beginning of the 13th century the Norman minster was considered unsuitable, and in 1220 work started on the present YORK MINSTER, which over a period of 250 years grew to be THE LARGEST GOTHIC CATHEDRAL IN NORTHERN EUROPE, 524 ft (160 m) in length and 249 ft (76 m) at its widest across the transepts. The nave

is THE WIDEST OF ANY MEDIEVAL
CATHEDRAL IN EUROPE and THE
SECOND TALLEST IN ENGLAND after
Westminster Abbey.

York Minster contains MORE
MEDIEVAL STAINED GLASS THAN ANY
OTHER CATHEDRAL IN BRITAIN and
includes BRITAIN'S OLDEST GLASS, part
of a Jesse window that dates from 1150.
THE GREAT EAST WINDOW, built by
JOHN THORNTON in 1405–8 is the
EARLIEST known ENGLISH WORK OF
ART BY A NAMED ARTIST. Covering over
2000 square feet (194 sq m) it is also
THE LARGEST EXPANSE OF MEDIEVAL
GLASS IN THE WORLD.

Medieval York

Within the city walls of York today
are many reminders of the medieval
city, as exemplified by its most famous
old street, the SHAMBLES, with its
overhanging timber-frame buildings,
regarded as THE BEST-PRESERVED
MEDIEVAL STREET IN EUROPE. The
name Shambles comes from the Saxon
'fleshammels', meaning meat shelves,
and signifies a street where meat is
sold. Alas, there are no butchers in
the Shambles today, but in nearby
Blossom Street can be found ROBERT
BURROW ATKINSON'S BUTCHER'S SHOP,
where the original YORK HAM was
conceived. The meat would be cured
for at least 12 months in the cellars
beneath the shop.

The EARLIEST EXAMPLES IN
ENGLAND OF OVERHANGING ARCHI-
TECTURE, where the upper storeys of
the buildings project out over the
street, can be found in LADY ROW, off
Goodramgate, where the cottages date
from 1320.

In Fossgate is York's grandest
medieval survival, the MERCHANT
ADVENTURERS' HALL, founded in 1357
and THE OLDEST GUILD HALL IN
BRITAIN. The hall itself is a paradise
of wood, with oak posts dividing the

room into two lengths and a superb wooden roof. The gatehouse is 17th-century and guards the entrance to THE MOST COMPLETE GROUP OF GUILD BUILDINGS IN EUROPE.

The Pricke of Conscience

Squeezed between modern hotels and some medieval cottages west of the Ouse is ALL SAINTS, NORTH STREET, originally a single Norman cell of 1089, added to over the years and now sporting a rather fine spire and octagonal belfry. The treasure of All Saints is a collection of 14th- and 15th-century stained glass to rival the minster, if not in quantity then most certainly in quality.

The most precious window, UNIQUE IN EUROPE, is the PRICKE OF CONSCIENCE WINDOW, at the east end of the north aisle, which dates from 1425 and portrays the final 15 days to the end of the world, expected then around 1500. The panels depict floods, earthquakes and fires, not unlike the scenarios predicted to ensue from global warming today. The penitent figures kneeling at the base of the window are thought to be members of the Henryson and Hessle families, who paid for the window in hope of salvation. This extraordinary wonder is the work of John Thornton, who designed the Great East Window in the minster, and is based on a poem by a 13th-century hermit, Richard of Hampole.

Haunted York

York is known as one of the most haunted cities in the world, and perhaps the most haunted house in York is the TREASURER'S HOUSE behind the minster, a restored Jacobean house built on top of the old Roman city. Roman soldiers are seen to march through the walls of the cellar, apparently cut off at the knees, but in fact walking along at the level of the old Roman road, which was discovered beneath the existing cellar floor during restoration work. The house stands on the site of the residence of the minster's treasurer, a position abolished at the Reformation. It was rebuilt in the early 17th century and then purchased in 1897 by an eccentric gentleman called FRANK GREEN, who refashioned the rooms to suit his extensive collection of antique furniture. He handed the house and contents over to the National Trust in 1930.

Georgian York

York has a number of fine Georgian houses, one of which, BAR CONVENT of 1787, houses THE OLDEST LIVING CONVENT IN ENGLAND, founded as a school, exclusively for females, in 1686.

MANSION HOUSE, which stands in front of the Guildhall, was built in 1729 and is the home of the mayor – it is THE ONLY MANSION HOUSE OUTSIDE THE CITY OF LONDON IN WHICH THE MAYOR ACTUALLY LIVES DURING HIS OF HER TERM OF OFFICE. Hanging above the stairwell is a large portrait of George Hudson, the controversial 'Railway King' to whom York owes its position as the premier railway hub in the North.

Victorian York

The story of Victorian York is one of railways and chocolate. York's Victorian railway station, with its magnificent curved glass and iron roof, had 13 platforms and was THE LARGEST STATION IN THE WORLD when completed in 1877. Adjoining the station is the NATIONAL RAILWAY MUSEUM, opened in 1925, THE FIRST AND LARGEST RAILWAY MUSEUM IN THE WORLD. Amongst its collection is the FLYING SCOTSMAN.

Chocolate York

TERRY'S OF YORK began life as Terry's and Berry's of York in 1823, when Pocklington-born apothecary JOSEPH TERRY joined the confectionery business of Robert Berry, who had a shop selling cough sweets close to Bootham Bar, in St Helen's Square. Not long afterwards Berry died and Terry was left running the business on his own. He decided to take advantage of York's position at the hub of the rail network and began to send his sweets all over Britain. When Joseph Terry died in 1850 his son, who was later knighted and became Mayor of York four times, took over and powered the company forward. The shop in St Helen's Square was kept as a retail outlet, but in 1926 Terry's moved to a purpose-built factory off Bishopthorpe Road, and it was here that some of their most popular brands came into the world – TERRY'S ALL GOLD in 1930 and TERRY'S CHOCOLATE ORANGE in 1931. In 1993 Terry's of York was taken over by Kraft, who closed the York factory in 2005 and moved production elsewhere.

BORN IN YORK

GUY FAWKES (1570–1606), Catholic revolutionary who attempted to blow up King James I and the Houses of Parliament on the night of 5 November 1605. He was born in High Petergate, baptised at St Michael le Belfrey and attended St Peter's School. His 'Gunpowder Plot' is commemorated every year on 5 November, Guy Fawkes Night.

JOSEPH ROWNTREE (1836–1925), Quaker philanthropist who took over his brother's chocolate business in York, in order to promote chocolate as a healthy alternative to alcohol for the working man. He eventually built the business into THE BIGGEST SWEET AND CHOCOLATE MANUFACTURER IN BRITAIN. In 1904 he established the JOSEPH ROWNTREE FOUNDATION, today a leading social policy research charity.

FRANKIE HOWERD (1917–92), comedian, favourite of the Queen Mother, perhaps best remembered for the television series *Up Pompeii*. His catchphrases included 'Titter ye not' and 'Oh no, missus, nooo'.

JOHN BARRY, film composer, born in 1933 and educated at St Peter's School. He wrote the music for the earlier James Bond films and won five Oscars, two for *Born Free* in 1966, and one each for *The Lion in Winter* (1968), *Out of Africa* (1985) and *Dances with Wolves* (1990).

DAME JUDI DENCH, actress, best known today for playing 'M' in the James Bond films and consistently voted Britain's favourite actress. In 1998 she won an Oscar for her portrayal of Queen Elizabeth I in *Shakespeare in Love*, although she appeared for only eight minutes – a tribute to her extraordinarily powerful presence on screen.

Ripon

Britain's Oldest City

RIPON IS THE OLDEST CITY IN BRITAIN. It was granted a charter by King Alfred the Great in 886 and presented with a horn as a symbol of the charter. At nine o'clock every night a wakeman, appointed by the people of Ripon to keep watch during the night hours, would sound the horn in Market Square to 'set the night watch', and although the wakeman was replaced by a mayor at the beginning of the 17th century, the tradition has been upheld for more than 1,100 years without a break. Today the Ripon Hornblower still sets the watch from the William Aislabie obelisk in the middle of Market

Square, in ONE OF THE OLDEST CERE-
MONIES PERFORMED IN ENGLAND.

St Wilfrid's Crypt

Even older is the simple crypt that
lies beneath the central tower of
Ripon's 12th-century cathedral. Just 11
ft (3.35 m) long and 8 ft (2.4 m) wide,
with a barrel roof and passages to
either side, the crypt was built by ST
WILFRID in 672, during the first
century of English Christianity. It has
survived invasions and sackings, as
well as the destruction and rebuilding of the cathedral above it, and
remains a rare place of extraordinary
peace and quiet, where all that has
gone on outside over the last 1,300
years seems to fade in importance.
For those in need of absolu-
tion, there is a narrow opening
known as ST WILFRID'S
NEEDLE, which is said to grant
forgiveness to any who can
scramble through it.

Fountains Abbey

Britain's Biggest Ruin

FOUNTAINS ABBEY, in the valley of
the River Skell south of Ripon, was
begun in 1132 by disgruntled Bene-
dictine monks from the abbey of St
Mary's in York, who defected to the
Cistercian Order. It was only THE
SECOND CISTERCIAN ABBEY BUILT IN
THE NORTH OF ENGLAND after
Rievaulx, which was begun two years
earlier, and grew to become the
LARGEST AND RICHEST CISTERCIAN
ABBEY IN BRITAIN. The remains of
Fountains now form THE LARGEST
MONASTIC RUINS IN BRITAIN.

The view from the west door down
the long narrow nave, 370 ft (113 m)
in length, towards the huge gaping
frame of the east window, is awe-
inspiring. Perhaps the most graceful
feature of the ruins is the CHAPEL OF
THE NINE ALTARS at the east end: a
rare place, as there is ONLY ONE OTHER
EXAMPLE OF A TRANSEPT AT THE EAST

END OF A CHURCH IN ENGLAND – at Durham Cathedral.

The most spectacular feature of the abbey buildings is the CELLARIUM, or storage area, a double avenue of vaulting, 300 ft (91 m) long, with pillars running down the centre from which stone ribs spring like the branches of a tree. It is THE LARGEST SUCH CELLARIUM SURVIVING IN EUROPE and, particularly when lit by the setting sun, it conveys a magical view of life in the 12th century.

The most dominant feature of Fountains Abbey is the great tower, 168 ft (51 m) high, and relatively new, having been put there by ABBOT MARMADUKE HUBY at the beginning of the 16th century, a fitting memorial to the most notable abbot of Fountains. The tower is unusual for a Cistercian house, as such ostentation was normally frowned upon by the Order.

At the Dissolution of the Monasteries, 400 years after it was begun, Fountains was sold to Sir Richard Gresham, father of the Thomas Gresham who founded the Royal Exchange in the City of London.

Fountains Hall

At the end of the 16th century the Fountains estate was sold to STEPHEN PROCTOR, who used stone from the abbey to build himself FOUNTAINS HALL, a little to the west of the ruins. This glorious Elizabethan house, which includes a banqueting hall with minstrel gallery, has passed through a number of hands over the years and been sadly neglected, apart from a brief heyday in the 1920s when Lady Doris Vyner, wife of the Marquess of Ripon, entertained royalty there. However, since the National Trust took it on in 1983 Fountains Hall has been slowly but painstakingly restored to its former majesty, and is now used as a spectacular venue for wedding receptions and parties.

Studley Royal

The STUDLEY ROYAL estate was inherited in 1699 by JOHN AISLABIE, first Tory Member of Parliament for Ripon, who was responsible for promoting the ill-fated South Sea Company, and who was then expelled from Parliament after the company's spectacular demise in the

South Sea Bubble of 1720. He turned his attention to creating a garden for his property at Studley Royal, and this was enhanced by his son William, who purchased the remains of Fountains Abbey and Fountains Hall, dammed the River Skel, and developed the grounds into THE FINEST GEORGIAN WATER GARDEN IN ENGLAND.

ST MARY'S CHURCH, in the deer park at Studley Royal, was designed by William Burges in 1870, and is considered to be his ecclesiastical masterpiece. It was commissioned by the Marchioness of Ripon to commemorate her brother, who was murdered by bandits in Greece.

In 1983 the whole estate was acquired by the National Trust, with the abbey ruins being managed by English Heritage on behalf of the Trust. In 1986 it was designated YORKSHIRE'S FIRST WORLD HERITAGE SITE.

Well, I never knew this about
YORK AND RIPON

On 25 August 1804 York racecourse hosted THE FIRST KNOWN HORSE RACE TO FEATURE A FEMALE JOCKEY COMPETING AGAINST A MALE JOCKEY, when ALICIA MEYNELL, riding Colonel Thornton's Vingarella side-saddle, took on Captain William Flint, riding Thornville, over 4 miles (6.4 km). Vingarella, a young horse, didn't complete the course, but Alicia Meynell returned the following year and rode the six-year-old Louisa against Frank Buckle on Allegro over 2 miles (3.2 km) – and won.

In 2008 York Minster became THE FIRST CATHEDRAL IN ENGLAND TO HAVE A CARILLON OF BELLS.

Leaning up against the west exterior wall of All Saints Church in North Street, York, is a tiny half-timbered house which claims to be THE SMALLEST HOUSE IN ENGLAND.

In 1723 Ripon racecourse hosted THE FIRST-EVER RACE FOR LADY RIDERS. The race was won by the local MP's wife, Mrs Aislabie.

The corn mill at Fountains Abbey is the ONLY 12TH-CENTURY CISTERCIAN CORN MILL LEFT IN BRITAIN and the oldest 'intact' building on the estate.

Moated MARKENFIELD HALL, 2 miles (3.2 km) south of Ripon, is THE MOST

COMPLETE SMALL 14TH-CENTURY COUNTRY HOUSE SURVIVING IN ENGLAND. Most of it was built in about 1310 by John Markenfield, Chancellor to Edward II, although the great hall dates from 1285. The Markenfields lost the estate after joining the Rising of the North in 1569, but after passing through a number of hands Markenfield is today once again owned by descendants of the Markenfields and is open to the public at certain times.

> The Rising of the North was a plot led by the Catholic northern earls, Charles Neville, Earl of Westmorland, and Thomas Percy, Earl of Northumberland, to overthrow Elizabeth I and put Mary Queen of Scots on the throne of England. As a result, the Nevilles lost Raby Castle and Northumberland was executed.

East Riding

BEVERLEY AND THE HUMBER

Beverley Minster – the most beautiful church in England?

Beverley

A Tale of Two Churches

BEVERLEY, capital of the East Riding, is as lovely as its name, with two glorious churches, and two ancient market-places joined by winding streets lined with gabled black-and-white houses and smart Georgian buildings. The streets and alleys follow the old courses of streams in which beavers once played – Beverley means 'beaver meadows'.

Beverley, which lies some 6 miles (9.6 km) upstream from Hull on the River Hull, grew up around the monastery founded here in the closing years of the 7th century by (SAINT) JOHN OF BEVERLEY, who was born in Harpham near the Holderness coast and rose to become Bishop of York. Amongst his pupils was the Venerable Bede, who later wrote of John's saintliness and erudition, and after John died in 721 his modest burial place in the monastic church at Beverley became a place of pilgrimage.

Sanctuary

Two hundred years later in 937 Alfred the Great's grandson KING ATHELSTAN came to pray at John's tomb on his way to battle and left a knife on the tomb, pledging to grant Beverley an endowment if he returned safely. He did return, having won a famous victory at the BATTLE OF BRUNAN-BURGH which made him King of All England, and the King not only granted Beverley an endowment but also the right of sanctuary – the Saxon sanctuary chair, or FRITH STOOL, given by Athelstan still sits by the altar and is ONE OF THE OLDEST IN EXISTENCE. Sanctuary extended for one mile from the church, and anyone who sat on the frith stool was granted 30 days' grace, during which time the church priests would try to mediate between the offender and his pursuers. If that failed then the offender would be escorted to the edge of town and handed over.

John was made a saint in 1037, and his remains were placed inside an

ornate shrine that attracted poor pilgrims and powerful ones – HENRY V came to Beverley to give thanks to St John for his victory at Agincourt in 1415.

The Most Beautiful Church in England?

The present Gothic minster was begun in 1220, after the tower of the Norman church collapsed. It took 200 years to build and is a supreme blend of all three Gothic styles, Early English, Decorated and Perpendicular. To many observers it is quite simply THE MOST BEAUTIFUL NON-CATHEDRAL CHURCH IN ENGLAND – and a fitting display of wealth for what was then the tenth richest town in the country. Particularly admired is the magnificent west front, with its two towers, said to be Hawksmoor's inspiration for the towers of Westminster Abbey.

Percy Tomb

The most elaborate of all the many treasures inside Beverley Minster is the PERCY TOMB, which was begun in 1340 and is thought to be that of Lady Eleanor Percy, who died in 1328 and was the wife of Henry Percy, the first Lord of Alnwick. The tomb itself is modest but the canopy is regarded as THE FINEST SURVIVING EXAMPLE OF 14TH-CENTURY GOTHIC CARVING IN ENGLAND – a feast of stone foliage and statues and sculptures.

Misericords and Music

Beverley Minster contains THE BIGGEST COLLECTION OF MISERICORDS OF ANY CHURCH IN ENGLAND, 68 of them, all richly carved with comic figures and tableaux. It also has THE LARGEST COLLECTION OF CARVINGS OF MEDIEVAL MUSICAL INSTRUMENTS IN THE WORLD, 70 of them in wood and stone, among them bagpipes, trumpets, tambourines, flutes and cymbals. And the central tower houses ENGLAND'S LARGEST SURVIVING MEDIEVAL TREADWHEEL CRANE – amazingly, it is still used.

St Mary's

A short walk away, past Wednesday Market, down Toll Gavel and through the spacious Saturday Market, is Beverley's other superb church, ST MARY'S, founded in the 12th century by the town's guildsmen. The impressive west front, built in about 1410, was the inspiration for King's College Chapel in Cambridge, which was begun about 30 years later. Much of

the rest of the church dates from the mid 16th century, the massive tower a replacement for one that fell down in 1520, killing a large number of the congregation.

The benefactors of the rebuilding are commemorated by a series of wonderful carvings on the nave pillars. The most striking of these is the MINSTREL PILLAR with its delightful group of five long-haired musicians in blue frock coats, holding medieval musical instruments. There are over 30

carvings with a musical theme in St Mary's, complementing the minster's world-beating collection, and joyously illustrating Beverley's links with the medieval Northern Guild of Minstrels.

One of the prominent merchants of St Mary's was Robert Fisher, father of (SAINT) JOHN FISHER (1469–1535), the Roman Catholic bishop who was executed by Henry VIII for failing to recognise the King as Head of the Church. John Fisher, THE ONLY MEMBER OF THE COLLEGE OF CARDINALS TO BE SO MARTYRED, was born in Flemingate in Beverley, and attended the BEVERLEY GRAMMAR SCHOOL, founded in AD 700 by John of Beverley and THE OLDEST STATE SCHOOL IN ENGLAND.

White Rabbit

There is one carving in St Mary's that is known way beyond Yorkshire, even beyond Britain. Little did the unsung medieval craftsman who carved the

perky rabbit above the door to the Sacristy know that 500 years later it would inspire a character beloved of children across the world. Charles Dodgson (Lewis Carroll), who had family in the East Riding and often visited Beverley as a youngster, discovered the rabbit in its hidden corner of the church, and later brought it to life as the WHITE RABBIT in ALICE IN WONDERLAND.

Hull

Shut against the King

HULL sits at the centre of THE THIRD LARGEST PORT COMPLEX IN BRITAIN after London and Liverpool, and was once THE BIGGEST FISHING PORT IN THE WORLD. It was founded in the 12th century by the monks from Meaux Abbey, 6 miles (9.6 km) away,

who built themselves a small quay at the point where the River Hull joins the Humber, from where they could ship the wool from their estates. In 1293 Edward I acquired the land and laid out the King's Town upon the Hull, or Kingston-upon-Hull as it is officially known.

The town started to really flourish when the richest merchant of the day, WILLIAM DE LA POLE, shifted his patronage from nearby Hedon, and was appointed as Hull's first mayor in 1331. De la Pole's descendants became the Earls of Suffolk, and he was THE FIRST MERCHANT EVER TO FOUND A NOBLE HOUSE.

In 1642 Hull was the scene of THE FIRST SKIRMISH OF THE ENGLISH CIVIL WAR, when on the orders of Parliament the Governor of Hull, SIR JOHN HOTHAM, shut the gates of the town against Charles I.

In 1778 THE FIRST ENCLOSED DOCK IN THE WORLD, THE QUEEN'S DOCK, was constructed in Hull, using THE WORLD'S FIRST BUCKET-CHAIN DREDGER to clear away the silt. In 1881 Hull's ALEXANDRA DOCK was THE FIRST DOCK IN THE WORLD TO BE BUILT USING A HYDRAULIC EXCAVATOR.

The Queen's Dock has now been filled in to provide a green open

William Wilberforce

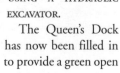

space, the Queen's Gardens, where a statue of Hull's most famous son, the anti-slavery campaigner William Wilberforce, stands on top of a pedestal 100 ft (30 m) high.

William Wilberforce

Wilberforce House

WILLIAM WILBERFORCE was born in a gloriously haphazard red-brick house in High Street in 1759, the son of a merchant and mayor of Hull made wealthy by the Baltic trade. Young Wilberforce was elected to Parliament at the age of 21, and his parliamentary career, as well as his life, culminated in perhaps the greatest political achievement of all time, the ABOLITION OF SLAVERY. He died in 1833 knowing that the cause for which he had so nobly fought would triumph one month later with the passing of the Slavery Abolition Act. His birthplace, Wilberforce House, is now a fascinating museum showcasing his life and work.

home of the Maister family who settled in Hull in the 16th century. It burned down in 1743, killing Henry Maister's wife and baby son, and was rebuilt in stone in 1744.

Close by is the WHITE HARTE INN, which contains a wood-panelled room called the PLOTTING PARLOUR, where Sir John Hotham and his associates met to agree the closing of the town gates against King Charles in 1642.

High Street, narrow, winding, dark, and swept by sea breezes, provides a wonderful evocation of what the old port of Hull must once have been like, and seems all the more atmospheric being surrounded by modern industrial devastation.

High Street

Wilberforce House stands at the northern end of the lovely cobbled HIGH STREET, which drunkenly follows the course of the River Hull and is lined with fine Georgian houses fronting old warehouses, many of which have been turned into museums. The splendidly Georgian MAISTER HOUSE, now owned by the National Trust, was the

Holy Trinity

Although Hull was, after London, the most heavily bombed place in Britain in the Second World War, with 95 per cent of the centre damaged or destroyed, some miracle preserved much of the heart of the old city, notably around HOLY TRINITY CHURCH, THE LARGEST PARISH

CHURCH IN ENGLAND and THE OLDEST BRICK BUILDING IN BRITAIN STILL SERVING ITS ORIGINAL PURPOSE. It dates from 1285 and was THE FIRST MAJOR BUILDING IN BRITAIN TO BE BUILT OF BRICK SINCE ROMAN DAYS. The guides in Holy Trinity are the funniest and most enthusiastic of any church in England, possibly because their remarkable church has such unprepossessing surroundings. They will lead you to the alleged tomb of Hull's first mayor, William de la Pole, point out the fantastical Victorian carvings on the pew ends, and encourage you to look for the seven trademark mice of Robert Thompson (*see* Kilburn, North York Moors) that are dotted throughout the church.

Across the square from Holy Trinity is the dignified 18th-century Trinity House, with its celebrated collection of Chippendale chairs. It was once the headquarters of the Guild of Pilots, who were responsible for the lightships on the Humber, but today administers marine charities and navigational schools. It is an oasis of calm in the middle of the city, with quiet courtyards and rooms full of books and rich mouldings.

Perhaps the most awe-inspiring building in the centre of Hull is the massive, pillared Edwardian Guildhall, which is 560 ft (171 m) long and takes up an entire block. It boasts a handsome clock tower and an array of noble statues.

The Deep

A walk along the riverfront at Hull is a bracing experience. Hull docks now spread for some 7 miles (11 km) along the banks of the Humber, and the quays by the city centre, where the ferries from Lincolnshire used to dock before the Humber Bridge was built, are all being redeveloped into offices, restaurants and flats. Situated right at the point where the Hull meets the Humber, on the site of the original abbey wharf, is a futuristic structure containing THE WORLD'S ONLY SUBMARIUM, a submerged aquarium called THE DEEP, which is said to be THE MOST SUCCESSFUL NATIONAL LOTTERY MILLENNIUM PROJECT IN BRITAIN.

R.I.P.

Dotted about the city are various memorials to Hull people who have died in unusual circumstances.

On the road to Hessle there is a statue of GEORGE SMITH, skipper of the fishing trawler *Crane*, who was killed in 1904 when the Russian fleet opened fire on a group of Hull trawlers fishing off the Dogger Bank, thinking they were Japanese torpedo boats. The *Crane* was sunk and three others were badly damaged.

In Hull cemetery there is a memorial to 44 airmen who died in 1921 when the *R38* airship, on a test flight out of Howden, broke up in mid-air and plunged into the Humber.

In Prospect Street there is a statue of Hull's most famous daughter, aviation pioneer AMY JOHNSON (1903–41), who was born in Hull and in 1930 became THE FIRST WOMAN TO FLY SOLO TO AUSTRALIA. In 1941 she disappeared after bailing out of her stricken aircraft over the River Thames in bad weather, and her body was never found.

The Royal Baccarat Scandal

On the western edge of Hull stands TRANBY CROFT, now a school, but once the scene of one of the biggest scandals of the 19th century. Tranby Croft, a large Victorian mansion, was the home of ARTHUR WILSON (1836–1909), owner of THE LARGEST PRIVATELY OWNED SHIPPING LINE IN THE WORLD, the WILSON LINE OF HULL.

One evening in 1890 Wilson played host at Tranby Croft to the

Prince of Wales, the future Edward VII, after the Prince had spent the day at Doncaster races. As the evening progressed the guests, including the Prince, began a game of baccarat, a card game where players gamble on who can get the nearest to the number nine with two cards. During the game some of the guests began to suspect Sir William Gordon-Cumming of cheating, and when the cheating continued the following evening they confronted Sir William and forced him to sign a document promising never to play cards again, even though he vehemently denied the accusation.

Although everyone had agreed to keep silent about the affair, the story got out and became the talk of London, and Sir William brought a libel action against his accusers to try and clear his name. This resulted in the Prince of Wales being called as a witness – a huge embarrassment for the royal family because baccarat was illegal in England.

Sir William lost his case, had to resign from the army and was ostracised from society. The reputation of the Wilson family was also tarnished and there were no more glittering royal occasions at Tranby Croft. The Wilson shipping fortunes eventually declined with the advent of air freight, and the house was sold in 1950.

Born in Hull

Famous natives of Hull are J. ARTHUR RANK (1888–1972), owner of Rank Hovis McDougall and founder of Pinewood Studios and the Rank Organisation entertainment company, and actors IAN CARMICHAEL (1920–2010), and MAUREEN LIPMAN, born in 1946.

Howden

Half a Church

HOWDEN is one of the East Riding's lost and ancient places, not as celebrated as it deserves to be, yet seemingly content to rest quietly beneath the tall, elegant tower of its minster, which overlooks the small market-place and forms the centrepiece of the town. The minster is still magnificent, despite only being half its original size – the chancel fell down in a storm in 1696 and was never rebuilt. Not long after that the late-14th-century OCTAGONAL CHAPTER HOUSE, THE LAST OF ITS KIND TO BE BUILT IN ENGLAND, also collapsed, and the ruins have now been interwoven into a delightfully imaginative garden. The mighty west end of the minster remains intact and is used as the parish church.

Horse Trading

In the 19th century Howden was renowned for hosting THE LARGEST HORSE FAIR IN BRITAIN (a distinction now held by Appleby in Westmoreland) and at that time, no doubt to cater for all those thirsty horse traders, the town boasted A GREATER CONCENTRATION OF PUBS THAN ANYWHERE ELSE IN ENGLAND.

Monarch of the Air

In 1915 the Admiralty opened an airship station at Howden to provide protection for the east coast ports, and by 1919 Howden had THE LARGEST AIRSHIP SHED IN THE WORLD, 750 ft (229 m) long and 130 ft (40 m) high.

In 1926 an engineer called Nevil Shute Norway, now better known as the author NEVIL SHUTE, came to lodge at No. 78 Hailgate in Howden

while working as chief stress engineer on the *R100* airship, which was being designed and built at the airship station by the Airship Guarantee Company, a subsidiary of Vickers. He is thought to have written his first novel, *Marazan*, while living in Howden.

The *R100* team was led by Barnes Wallis, who later invented the bouncing bomb used by the Dambusters in the Second World War, and the *R100* was a brilliant achievement, making a successful flight to Canada in August 1930. Unfortunately she was deflated and retired later that same year after her sister ship the *R101*, made at Cardington in Bedfordshire, crashed in France while on its way to India, with huge loss of life. Britain's enthusiasm for airships petered out and Howden airship station was closed shortly afterwards.

Paull

Of Blackburns and Bullocks

One of the best viewpoints for observing the activity on the Humber is the balcony of the little white lighthouse on the corner of the road in PAULL, a bracing village that lies beside the estuary about 5 miles (8 km) east of Hull. Built in 1836, the lighthouse is now a private residence.

A little further on down the river is FORT PAULL, originally built by Henry VIII to defend the Humber ports. It was rebuilt several times, lastly in 1862, but was closed in 1960, and is now a heritage museum. Among the exhibits is THE LAST SURVIVING EXAMPLE OF A BLACKBURN BEVERLEY, a heavy transport aircraft built further up the Humber at Brough in the 1950s.

Standing alone in a field a mile or so beyond Paull Church is a ruined 15th-century brick tower, all that is left of a large moated house called the Holmes, built in 1438 for John Holme and his new wife Elizabeth Wasteneys by John's father Robert Holme. The tower is said to be haunted by the ghost of a startled bullock, which ran up the stairs on to the roof and plunged over the parapet to its death.

Hotham

An Old Warhorse

Sir John Hotham, the Governor of Hull who closed the city gates to Charles I, got his family name from the village of HOTHAM, which lies at the foot of the Wolds some 10 miles (16 km) west of Hull.

A board on the gates of the driveway for HOTHAM HALL reads 'Ypres 347 miles', and below are recorded the number of casualties suffered at Ypres in the First World War. This very personal memorial was put there by a previous owner of the hall, Colonel Tom Clitherow, who fought at Ypres and was deeply moved by the carnage.

Hidden behind a hedge in the lovely grounds of Hotham Hall is the poignant gravestone of Colonel Clitherow's war horse, which bears the inscription:

IN MEMORY OF
A GALLANT
HORSE
BRED IN HOLDERNESS AND
HUNTED HERE HE LANDED
IN FRANCE 15 AUGUST 1914
MONS LE CATEAU AISNE
YPRES THE SOMME CAMBRAI
HE KNEW THEM ALL
AND NOW LIES HERE

Well, I never knew this about

BEVERLEY AND THE HUMBER

With a centre span of 4,626 ft (1,410 m), the HUMBER BRIDGE was THE LONGEST SUSPENSION BRIDGE IN THE WORLD for 16 years from its completion in 1981 until 1997, when it was overtaken by the Great Belt Bridge in Denmark. It is still THE LONGEST BRIDGE IN THE WORLD THAT CAN BE CROSSED ON FOOT. As a result of the earth's curvature, the towers are 1.4 inches (36 mm) further apart at the top than at the bottom.

THE HUMBER is not truly a river but a tidal estuary that begins at the confluence of two rivers, the Trent and the Ouse.

In 1931 Yorkshireman TED WRIGHT uncovered the remains of a wooden boat sunk into the muddy shoreline of the Humber at NORTH FERRIBY. It was found to be about 4,000 years old and from the Bronze Age. Nine years later he came across an even older boat just upstream, and a third was found next to the original in 1963. These three Bronze Age boats are THE OLDEST BOATS EVER DISCOVERED IN EUROPE.

BROUGH, which lies on the Roman road from York to Lincoln, sits on the site of the important Roman settlement of Petuaria, which was built to guard the river crossing into Lincolnshire. In 1916 the BLACKBURN AEROPLANE AND MOTOR COMPANY opened a new factory at Brough, which still operates today as part of BAE Systems. In the 1950s Brough became famous for manufacturing a new kind of fighter-bomber called the BLACKBURN BUCCANEER, which was produced there for 20 years and continued in service until the first Gulf War in 1991. Today the factory produces the HAWK, as used by the Red Arrows, the RAF's aerobatic display team.

The notorious highwayman DICK TURPIN, who lived in Yorkshire for some years under the name John Palmer, saw his last hours of freedom at the GREEN DRAGON INN in WELTON, where he was arrested in 1739, completely drunk, for horse stealing. His true identity was discovered while he was in gaol and he was sentenced to death for murder and hanged at York racecourse later that year.

Hull is THE ONLY CITY IN BRITAIN WITH ITS OWN INDEPENDENTLY OPERATED TELEPHONE SYSTEM, KINGSTON COMMUNICATIONS, which took over the system from Hull City Council in 2007, and THE ONLY CITY IN BRITAIN TO HAVE WHITE TELEPHONE BOXES.

Hull can boast of having THE FIRST WOMAN PHOTOGRAPHER IN BRITAIN, a MRS ANN COOK, who set up a portrait studio at No. 6 George Street in 1845.

In 1928 ELASTOPLAST was invented in Hull by Thomas James Smith and his nephew Horatio of SMITH AND NEPHEW, dispensing chemists of Hull since 1865.

The poet PHILIP LARKIN (1922–85) is buried in the cemetery at COTTINGHAM on the edge of Hull. Cottingham claims to be THE BIGGEST VILLAGE IN ENGLAND.

HOLDERNESS AND THE COAST

St Augustine's Church, Hedon, the King of Holderness

The King and Queen of Holderness

Holderness is graced by two of the finest churches in England. One is rugged and sturdy, the other light and graceful, and together they are known as the 'King and Queen of Holderness'.

The King

THE 'KING' is the church of ST AUGUSTINE, which broods over the little town of HEDON, just to the east of Hull. Hedon was founded after the Norman Conquest by the Earl of Albemarle, and during the 12th century was a flourishing port, reached by a small inlet from the Humber. St Augustine's Church was begun in 1180 to serve what was then the most important port on the Humber, and grew into a splendid structure of cathedral-like proportions, crowned with a magnificent 14th-century Perpendicular tower, 130 ft (40 m) high, that can still be seen from miles around.

Alas, Hedon's inlet began to silt up, and during the late 13th and early 14th centuries trade gradually slipped away west, to a new port being developed at the mouth of the River Hull by an enterprising merchant called William de la Pole (*see* Hull). Hedon slowly sank back into the marshes and became a sleepy backwater. Today it is overshadowed by Hull's fearsome chemical installations and gas plants that loom and wink mockingly from across the flat fields.

Hedon declined to join in such tasteless industrial expansion and instead slumbered aloof beneath the watchful eye of St Augustine. After a fire destroyed much of the town in 1656, Hedon evolved into a place of genteel, if somewhat dilapidated, Georgian streets and quiet cobbled corners, where time seems to falter and often come to a complete stop. Somehow, though, one gets the feeling that the 'King', hunched, lonely and neglected as he may be now, will still reign over Holderness long after the industrial chimneys of Hull are razed to the ground and forgotten.

The Queen

Some 10 miles (16 km) to the southeast, THE 'QUEEN OF HOLDERNESS', ST PATRICK'S CHURCH in PATRINGTON, shimmers in the pale watery light of the Humber where it melts into the bleak North Sea. Here, as in chess, the Queen is taller and more flamboyant than the King, her consort in Hedon, and this Queen, honey-coloured and flecked with silver, is regarded by many as THE MOST PERFECT VILLAGE CHURCH IN ENGLAND. Her slender spire, 189 ft (58 m) high, soars in breathtaking beauty above the bare, far eastern fields and has been a landmark since it was raised in the 14th century. Captain Bligh (of the *Bounty*) used it as a reference point when he was conducting a nautical survey of the Humber.

The church was built almost entirely in the first half of the 14th century, before the Black Death struck and brought such work to a halt, and thus has a harmony of style and proportion that is deeply satisfying. The interior possesses 30 graceful arches on clustered columns and a wealth of rich stone carving, including some 200 human and animal faces. There is also a rare surviving example of an EASTER SEPULCHRE, and the tomb of Robert de Patrington, master mason at York Minster from 1369, who is thought to be largely responsible for the creation of this sublime masterpiece. The 'Queen of Holderness' is a remarkable treasure to find in such a distant, lonely place, but when the church was built, Patrington stood in the heart of rich farmland and was an important staging post on the road from York and Hedon to the busy port of Ravenser Odd, which stood on a sand spit at the mouth of the Humber near what is known today as Spurn Head.

Spurn Head

Shifting Sands

SPURN HEAD is a thin tongue of land made up of shingle and sand that juts out for 3½ miles (5.6 km) into the mouth of the Humber. Every 250 years or so the spit gets washed away, along with any settlements that have sprung

---

An EASTER SEPULCHRE is an arched recess normally found in the north wall of the chancel in a church, beside the altar, where the crucifix and other sacred elements of the Easter story are placed during the Easter period, from Good Friday to Easter Day. FOUND ONLY IN ENGLAND, they were usually made of wood, but there are a number of examples in stone, although these are rare, most being destroyed during the Reformation or Civil War. The Easter Sepulchre at Patrington is considered amongst the finest, with its exquisitely carved Roman soldiers guarding the tomb, and Jesus emerging from the tomb flanked by angels.

up along its shore, and then reforms a few yards to the west, where it becomes established again for another 250 years. In the late 13th century the spit was in the middle of its cycle and the shoreline was firm enough for a small port to develop near the point – this was RAVENSER ODD, which expanded rapidly and became important enough to be represented at the Model Parliament of 1295.

Such was its strategic importance that Ravenser Odd saw much excitement during its short existence. In the summer of 1332 EDWARD BALLIOL came to Ravenser Odd with a small army, and then set sail for Scotland on his quest to wrest his father's crown from the House of Bruce. In 1399 HENRY BOLINGBROKE, DUKE OF LANCASTER, landed at Ravenser Odd on his return from exile, and from here marched on London where he deposed Richard II and was crowned as Henry IV.

By the start of the 15th century Ravenser Odd had pretty much disappeared and its trade had moved west along the Humber to a safer haven at Hull. In March 1471 the Yorkist EDWARD IV landed near what was left of Ravenser Odd, close to where the Lancastrian Bolingbroke had come ashore 72 years earlier, and began his own march to London to reclaim his throne from the Lancastrian Henry VI. It would seem that the shifting fortunes of the Wars of the Roses had their origins on the shifting sands of Spurn Head.

The stone cross that was erected on the spot where Henry Lancaster and Edward York landed was long ago rescued from the encroaching sea, and now stands in the garden of an old people's home in Hedon.

To the Point

Spurn Head today is a wild and windswept place, but not quite as devoid of human life as you might expect, given that the lighthouse on the Point has been disused since 1986. Pilots race out from a jetty at Spurn Point to assist ships wishing to navigate the hazardous channels of the Humber estuary, one of the world's busiest waterways, and there is also a lifeboat station there which is home to BRITAIN'S ONLY FULL-TIME PAID LIFEBOAT CREW. Most of Spurn Head now belongs to the Yorkshire Wildlife Trust, but for a small fee you can drive along the narrow road to the Point, where you can breathe in the bracing sea breezes, observe the varied bird-life or watch the constant comings and goings of the huge ships passing by.

Winestead

Nestling amongst a grove of trees, at the end of a short, concealed track off the main road to Patrington, is one of

Yorkshire's secret churches, the tiny, towerless 12th-century church of ST GERMAIN, WINESTEAD. In the undergrowth behind the church is a deep ditch, all that remains of a huge square moat that surrounded the old manor house whose foundations lie beneath the grass in the enclosed field beyond the ditch. The house was pulled down in 1579 by SIR CHRISTOPHER HILDYARD after his son was drowned in the moat.

Sir Christopher, whose family had owned the manor of Winestead since the days of Richard II, is buried inside the church, in a great chest tomb in front of the pulpit. His melancholy figure, clad in armour, hands clasped in prayer, lies on a mattress on top of the tomb, and the date of his death, 1602, is engraved on the side.

The cluttered interior of the church was re-organised in Jacobean style by the Victorian architect Temple Moore at the end of the 19th century, but still in place at the west end is the medieval font where, in 1621, the poet, patriot and Parliamentarian Andrew Marvel was baptised by his father, who was the Rector.

represent as its Member of Parliament for 33 years. He was a popular and incorruptible MP, a staunch friend to Oliver Cromwell and much admired by Charles II, but he is even more fondly remembered as a great poet. The lines he wrote on the death of Charles I are amongst his best known:

'He nothing common did or mean
Upon that memorable scene,
But with his keener eye,
The axe's edge did try;
Nor called the Gods with vulgar spite
To vindicate his helpless right,
But bowed his comely head
Down, as upon a bed.'

Marvellous

ANDREW MARVEL was born in the Rectory at Winestead, but he was only three years old when his family moved down the road to Hull, the city that Andrew would eventually go on to

Burton Constable

A Whale of a Time

The grandest house in Holderness, the pink-brick, Elizabethan, BURTON CONSTABLE HALL, is set in beautiful

parkland landscaped by Capability Brown, and has been the home of the Constable family for more than 400 years. The Constables still live in one wing, and the rooms in the main part of the house are finely decorated in a variety of period styles, but the house is so big and rambling that it reeks of adventure. Everywhere there are sudden, tantalising glimpses of dusty, dim-lit corridors leading off to who knows where, entrances to unseen stairways that spiral up through ghostly towers, and provocatively locked doors that must surely conceal rooms untouched for generations and filled with family skeletons . . .

Talking of skeletons, during the 19th century the skeleton of a 60 ft (18 m) whale was displayed in the park, supported on an iron frame. It had been discovered on the coast near Tunstall in 1825 and was brought to Burton Constable because the Constables, as Lords of the Seigniory of Holderness, were entitled to anything of interest that was washed up on the Holderness coast. The skeleton caused great excitement as nobody had really had the chance to study a whale before, and the specimen was dissected and pored over by a number of eminent personages. The American writer Herman Melville was fascinated when he read about it and used the Burton Constable whale as his inspiration for the whale MOBY DICK in his classic novel published in 1851.

The remains of the skeleton have recently been recovered from the park, and it is hoped that the 'Moby Dick' whale can soon be put on public display once more.

Withernsea

A Tale of Two Stars

The little seaside town of Withernsea on the Holderness coast was the birthplace of two renowned artists, whose most memorable performances turned out to be with each other. They were . . .

KENNY BAKER (1921–99), regarded by many as the best English jazz trumpeter of all time. After being lead trumpeter for the Ted Heath Band after the Second World War, he went on to form his own jazz band, Baker's Dozen, in the 1950s. He later appeared with many top entertainers such as Morecambe and Wise, Benny Hill and Ken Dodd, accompanied Frank Sinatra and Tony Bennett, amongst others, and also provided music for a number of television programmes including the *Beiderbecke* trilogy and *The Muppet Show*. His best-known soundtrack was a long trumpet solo mimed by Kay Kendall (*see* below) in the 1953 film *Genevieve*.

KAY KENDALL (1926–59), actress, was born Justine Kendall McCarthy in Withernsea. Remembered equally for her beauty and her comic timing, she starred in several successful films including *Genevieve*, in which she

mimed to a trumpet solo performed by fellow Withernsea native Kenny Baker (*see* above). In 1954 she appeared in *Doctor in the House* with Dirk Bogarde and the following year in *The Constant Husband* alongside Rex Harrison, whom she later married. In 1958 she won a Golden Globe Award for her performance in the film *Les Girls*. She died of leukaemia in 1959 at the age of 33.

Bridlington

Look West

The restored Perpendicular west window of BRIDLINGTON PRIORY is THE LARGEST WEST WINDOW IN THE NORTH OF ENGLAND. In medieval days Bridlington Priory, founded in 1113, was the grandest church in Yorkshire after York Minster, until the last prior joined the Pilgrimage of Grace and lost his head. His priory suffered too, with only the nave surviving to serve as the parish church of St Mary. Today the church, still impressive, slumbers in the quiet of Old Bridlington's 17th-century High Street, far away from the candyfloss and kiss-me-quick of New Bridlington's seaside. Across the gardens of Church Green from the priory is the 14th-century priory gatehouse, known as Bayle Gate, which now houses a museum of local antiquities.

St John of Bridlington, Prior of Bridlington from 1362 until his death in 1379, was canonised in 1401 by Pope Boniface IX as THE LAST ENGLISH SAINT TO BE CANONISED BEFORE THE REFORMATION.

Filey

Brigg Ahoy!

Filey sits on the boundary between the North and East Ridings of Yorkshire, which until 1974 ran along the bottom of the ravine that separates the church in the North from the village in the East. This division gave rise to the local saying 'He'll soon be in the North Riding', referring to someone very ill and not expected to recover.

Filey was originally a small fishing village that evolved in Victorian times into a seaside resort for those who wished to escape from the bustle and crowds of Scarborough. It sits above

6 miles (9.6 km) of golden sands, protected from the north by a long, low finger of rock called FILEY BRIGG, which juts out into the North Sea for almost a mile, acting as a natural breakwater. At low tide there are adventurous walks along the Brigg, winding through rock pools and sea spray, and offering fine views north to Scarborough Castle and south to Flamborough Head. At high tide the Brigg becomes submerged, and over the years many ships have been lost on the hidden reefs. The seabed around is littered with wrecks, making Filey Bay a popular destination for divers and treasure seekers.

Battle of Flamborough Head

Birthplace of the American Navy

The most highly sought-after wreck in Filey Bay is not a treasure ship, nor a victim of the Brigg, but a casualty of one of the most significant battles of the American War of Independence, the BATTLE OF FLAMBOROUGH HEAD. On the evening of 23 September 1779, a small squadron of the American Continental Navy, donated by the French and led by the Scots-born American privateer JOHN PAUL JONES, engaged two British warships which were escorting the Baltic merchant fleet down the Yorkshire coast to Hull.

The battle, watched from the cliffs by people from Scarborough to Flamborough, was brutal and fierce, the sea foaming red with blood and many dead and mutilated on both sides. The lead British ship HMS *Serapis* and Jones's ship BONHOMME RICHARD (named in honour of Jones's patron Benjamin Franklin who wrote a popular almanac under the name of 'Poor Richard') became locked together and caught fire. After a mighty explosion rocked the *Bonhomme Richard*, the watchers on the cliff thought that Jones was lost, his ship dismasted and his flag shot away. Captain Pearson is said to have called on Jones to surrender, but Jones's reply, 'I have not yet begun to fight,' has become part of American Navy folklore.

In the end it was the British commander Captain Pearson who, to save further slaughter, and once he was satisfied that the convoy had escaped to the safety of the harbour at Scarborough, surrendered his sword

to Jones on board the *Bonhomme Richard*.

Once Jones realised his beloved flagship could not be saved, he boarded the *Serapis* with his crew and set sail for neutral Holland, where he handed over his prize and its crew to the French, and took command of a new American ship, the *Alliance*. The *Bonhomme Richard* was left drifting out to sea, to sink slowly beneath the waves some two days later.

Although the battle was small in terms of the number of ships involved, John Paul Jones's perceived success against the might of the Royal Navy helped to secure French support for the American Revolution – support that would prove decisive in the American colonies' battle for independence from Britain.

The Hunt is On

There have been many attempts to locate the wreck of the now legendary *Bonhomme Richard* over the years. In 1975 a diver from Filey, John Adams, found the remains of a wooden vessel dating from between 1776 and 1800 out in the bay, since which time several British and American teams, one led by the American crime writer CLIVE CUSSLER, have been in a race to discover if this promising find actually is the long lost flagship of the 'Father of the American Navy'.

Flamborough

Toad in the Hole

The most interesting tomb in the Norman church of St Oswald in Flamborough is that of 'Little' Sir Marmaduke Constable, who died in agony from swallowing a toad while drinking a glass of water. The toad proceeded to gnaw its way out by eating Sir Marmaduke's heart. This cautionary tale is graphically illustrated on the tomb by a sculpture showing the ribcage laid open to reveal a bulbous heart.

Before his unfortunate end, Sir Marmaduke would go every Christmas to Flamborough Head and fire an arrow with a gold coin attached to it out to sea and call for the King of the Danes to come and collect it – his reasoning being that the Constables had been prominent in Flamborough for so long that they no longer knew who to pay their rent to. Flamborough is thought to have been founded by the Danes and lies at the centre of an area known as Little Denmark.

Sir Marmaduke fought at the Battle of Flodden in 1513 at the age of 70. His son Robert, who was with him at Flodden, later joined the Pilgrimage of Grace in 1536 and was executed in Hull.

Well, I never *knew this*
about
HOLDERNESS AND THE COAST

Hedon possesses THE OLDEST CIVIC MACE IN ENGLAND. It was presented to the town in 1415 during the reign of Henry V.

Hedon Park Racecourse, laid out in fields to the west of Hedon in 1888, boasted THE LONGEST RACING 'STRAIGHT' IN BRITAIN. After 1910 the straight found a new use as an airstrip and many of the early pioneers of aviation came to Hedon to practise their skills. In 1930, not long after her epic flight to Australia, local heroine Amy Johnson landed at Hedon in front of a huge and enthusiastic crowd. After the Second World War the course functioned briefly as a speedway track, but the site has long since reverted to green fields – although it is reported that some still use it as an unofficial motorcycle racetrack . . .

KILNSEA, just to the north of Spurn Head, is THE EASTERNMOST VILLAGE IN YORKSHIRE. The Bluebell Inn in Kilnsea was 534 yards (488 m) from the sea when it was built in 1847. Today it is less than 150 yards (137 m) from the sea.

NORTH SEA GAS FIRST CAME ASHORE AT THE EASINGTON GAS TERMINAL, in 1967. The terminal lies 1 mile (1.6 km) north of the village of Easington on the Holderness coast, north of Spurn Head. The Easington terminal now stands at one end of THE WORLD'S LONGEST UNDERSEA PIPELINE, the BRITPIPE or LANGELED pipeline, 725 miles (1,166 km) in length, which links the Nyhamna terminal in Norway to Easington via the Sleipner Riser North Sea gas field.

EASINGTON village is home to the EASINGTON IMP, carved on the tower arch of the 12th-century church, and also to THE ONLY SURVIVING MEDIEVAL THATCHED TITHE BARN IN THE EAST RIDING.

The PRIME MERIDIAN departs Britain at SAND LE MERE near the tiny village of Tunstall, on the Holderness coast. This is also THE NORTHERNMOST PIECE OF LAND ON THE ENTIRE LENGTH OF THE PRIME MERIDIAN.

HORNSEA MERE, which lies west of Hornsea, and is just 2 miles (3.2 km) from the sea, is THE LARGEST FRESH-WATER LAKE IN YORKSHIRE. It is 2 miles long, up to ¾ mile (1.2 km) wide and a maximum of 12 feet (3.6 m) deep.

The small bellcote church of ST JAMES IN LISSETT houses a bell inscribed with the date 1254, THE OLDEST DATED BELL IN BRITAIN. Lissett was the site of an important airfield for Halifax bombers during the Second World War.

LEO BLAIR, father of former Prime Minister Tony Blair, was born in FILEY in 1923, the illegitimate son of two actors, Charles Parsons and Celia Ridgway.

THE FIRST PASSENGER TO DIE IN A PLANE CRASH IN ENGLAND lost his life on FILEY SANDS, when his plane came down there in 1911, killing both the passenger and the pilot.

The octagonal chalk tower on FLAM- BOROUGH HEAD, erected in 1673, is claimed to be THE OLDEST SURVIVING LIGHTHOUSE IN ENGLAND.

It was off Flamborough Head that Prince James Stewart, son of Robert III of Scotland, was captured by the English in 1406, while trying to escape to France. From here he was sent to Windsor, where he was held prisoner for 19 years, during which time he fell in love with Joan Beaufort, the niece of Henry IV. James married Joan in London in 1423 and took her home to Scotland as his Queen when he ascended the Scottish throne as James I the following year.

Many of J.R.R. TOLKEIN's tales of Middle Earth were inspired by walks along the Holderness coast with his wife Edith, who 'danced among the hemlocks'. In 1917 Tolkein was posted to ROOS and put in charge of a battalion outpost guarding the Holderness coast, while he was convalescing from trench fever caught at the Somme.

The BEMPTON CLIFFS form THE LARGEST BREEDING GROUND FOR BIRDS ON THE ENGLISH MAINLAND and are also THE SITE OF THE ONLY MAINLAND GANNETRY IN GREAT BRITAIN.

Yorkshire Wolds

*Sledmere House, the first country house
to have its interior photographed by* Country Life

Sledmere

Order out of Chaos

Before the Sykes family arrived, the YORKSHIRE WOLDS were, according to Daniel Defoe, writing in 1727, 'very thin of towns and people'. Nothing prospered or grew on the bare, desolate hills except wolves, who prowled the Wolds until well into the 17th century.

In 1751 RICHARD SYKES, a wealthy Hull merchant whose father had married the heir to the SLEDMERE estates, decided he wanted to improve his property, so he demolished the run-down Tudor manor house and, on 17 April 1751, 'laid the first stone of the new house at Sledmere'. He planted 20,000 trees, created hedgerows and began to transform the barren wilderness into some of the most productive agricultural land in England. His nephew SIR CHRISTOPHER SYKES, who inherited Sledmere in 1776, and also married well, commissioned Capability Brown to design a 2,000-acre (800 ha) park, and replaced the old village of Sledmere with a new model village for his estate workers.

A Library and a Turkish Room

In 1911 Sledmere House was gutted by fire, with just the four walls left standing, but it was swiftly rebuilt using the original plans and to the same Georgian design. The LIBRARY, beautifully restored in blue, white and gold by the present owner SIR TATTON SYKES, 8TH BARONET, is one of the most beautiful rooms in England. Running the whole length of the house, it is 120 ft (37 m) long and boasts a glorious vaulted ceiling based on the baths of ancient Rome. One of the most unusual rooms to be found in the house – or in any stately home – is the TURKISH ROOM. It was designed for diplomat Sir Mark Sykes by Armenian artist David Ohaness-ian, built from tiles made in Damascus, and is based on a sultan's apartment in the Valideh Mosque in Istanbul. A visit to Sledmere, when the great pipe organ under the stairs is playing full blast, conjuring up visions of Count Dracula and his organ rising from the basement, is an unforgettable experience.

In 1897 Sledmere became THE FIRST COUNTRY HOUSE TO HAVE ITS INTERIOR PHOTOGRAPHED BY *COUN-TRY LIFE* MAGAZINE.

Old Tat

In common with so many noble families, the Sykes family have been blessed with their fair share of characters. SIR TATTON SYKES, 4TH BARONET (1772–1863), known as 'OLD TAT', was described as 'one of the three sights of Yorkshire', along with York Minster and Fountains Abbey. A renowned sportsman, jockey and pugilist, he used the library for physical rather than mental exercise, rising at 5.30 every morning and striding up and down the room for 4 miles (6.4 km) before enjoying a light breakfast washed down with a glass of stout and double cream. Although his father Sir Christopher is credited with being the 'Reformer of the Wolds', Sir Tatton was likewise an innovative agriculturalist, and was responsible for THE DISCOVERY OF BONEMEAL AS A FERTILISER – having noticed that the grass where his foxhounds had gnawed at their bones was more lush.

Despite living most of his life in the 19th century, Sir Tatton Sykes remained at heart a puritanical 18th-century gentleman. He dressed as such, and brought up his children in spartan 18th-century style – plenty of cold baths and discipline – but his workers adored him because he treated everyone the same.

In 1865 a tall stone monument, 120 ft (37 m) high, was built on a hilltop above Sledmere in memory of Sir Tatton. It bears the inscription, 'Erected to the memory of Sir Tatton Sykes, Baronet, by those who loved him as a friend and honoured him as a landlord'. A staircase spirals up the inside to a small room from which there are panoramic views across the Wolds in all directions. Alas, for reasons of health and safety, the monument is no longer open.

Milk Pudding

Not surprisingly, the 4th baronet's son and heir, SIR TATTON SYKES, 5TH BARONET (1826–1913), was a slightly withdrawn individual with a passion for milk puddings. When going out for a walk he would put on several overcoats and trousers, which he would then proceed to peel off as he got warmer with exercise – the discarded items being picked up by a

servant trailing in his wake. When informed that Sledmere had gone up in flames, he was immersed in milk pudding, and waved the impertinent messenger away with the words 'First, I must finish my pudding, finish my pudding . . . '

Sykes Churches Trail

Between them the Sir Tatton Sykes-es, 4th and 5th baronets, financed the sympathetic restoration of a huge number of local churches, working with distinguished architects such as J.L. Pearson (Truro Cathedral), G.E. Street (Royal Courts of Justice) and Temple Moore. One of the most spectacular of these churches can be found in the neighbouring village of GARTON-ON-THE-WOLDS, near the Sykes monument, where G.E. Street supervised the redecoration of the interior of the sturdy Norman church with a riot of colourful murals and mosaics. The walls of the nave are completely covered with scenes from the Old Testament, the chancel walls with stories from the New Testament, and the floor picked out in mosaics of black and white and yellow. The whole effect is breathtaking.

To the north, at KIRBY GRINDA-LYTHE, G.E. Street has covered the whole west wall of the church with a vast, golden mosaic showing the Ascension of Our Lord – an extraor-dinary sight to find in a Yorkshire

Garton-on-the-Wolds

country church. All of the churches restored by the Sykeses can be visited on the SYKES CHURCHES TRAIL, details of which can be found at Sledmere or local visitor centres.

Sykes of Arabia

SIR MARK SYKES, 6TH BARONET (1879–1919), was a brilliant writer and politician who travelled widely, especially in the Middle East. During the build-up to the Great War he formed the WAGGONERS SPECIAL RESERVE, a unit that drew its recruits from the farm workers of the Wolds and other rural areas. Sir Mark reckoned that their expertise at driving farm wagons in difficult conditions would prove invaluable in getting men and equipment to the front line, and so it proved. There is a memorial to the Waggoners, designed by Sir Mark, in the village at Sledmere.

In 1915 Sir Mark joined Lord Kitchener's War Office with special responsibility for the Middle East. In this role he instigated the Arab Bureau, which had amongst its members T.E. Lawrence and Gertrude Bell, and helped co-ordinate the Arab fight against the Ottoman Empire. He was responsible for designing the Flag of Arab Revolt, a combination of black, white, green and red that today forms the basis of many of the flags of the modern Arab states. In 1916 he negotiated the controversial Sykes-Picot Agreement, a secret agreement between Britain and France laying out their respective spheres of influence after the expected collapse of the Ottoman Empire.

In 1919 Sir Mark travelled to France to take part in the peace negotiations, but contracted Spanish flu and died in his hotel room at the age of 39. He was brought back to Sledmere in a lead-lined coffin and buried in the graveyard of St Mary's Church, adjoining the big house.

Body of Evidence

Sir Mark Sykes's remarkable legacy could turn out to be even more significant than the modern-day map of the Middle East – it may be able to save the world. In 2007, 88 years after it was laid to rest, Sir Mark's body was exhumed so that scientists could try to extract samples of the flu virus that had killed him, believed to be similar to the bird flu virus of concern to the world today. Because his body had lain in a lead-lined coffin it was very well preserved, and the hope of scientists is that they may be able to learn from the samples taken from Sir Mark how to create an antidote.

Londesborough

Paradise on Earth

On a visit in 1665, James II, then Duke of York, described LONDESBOROUGH as 'a paradise on earth'. It still is.

The view from the crossroads above the village takes in the silvery Humber with Lincolnshire beyond, the Vale of York, the West Riding and great swathes of rolling Wolds. The village nestles in a dip, with little red-roofed cottages and an ancient church all surrounded by parkland dotted with trees and avenues and terraces. The church has a doorway built by the Normans, above which is an Anglo-Danish cross and sundial from the 10th century.

The Dawn of Christian England

James II was not the first of royal blood to appreciate the beauty of this place. The Saxon King Edwin of Northumbria had a summer palace here, and in AD 627 he hosted a Great Council to discuss whether to adopt Christianity or to continue with the old pagan ways.

On the Christian wing was Paulinus, emissary of the Pope, and Edwin's Queen, Ethelberta, daughter of the Christian Queen Bertha of Kent. Of the pagan persuasion were the King's hardened warriors and his Chief Priest, COIFI. Edwin himself was resistant to change, and the debate was deadlocked, when an old man rose from the back of the hall and began to talk.

'The life of man,' he said, 'is like a sparrow that flies out of the night into a brightly lit hall, tarries for a moment, and then flies out of the other door back into the dark. What is before us and what lies after we do not know. If this new doctrine will tell us anything of these mysteries, let us follow it.'

Such was the power of his words that Edwin was decided, and so was his Chief Priest. 'I have worshipped the pagan gods all my life and they have not made me rich,' Coifi declared. Then, with the blessing of his King, Coifi leaped on to his horse and rode like the wind down to GOODMANHAM, where the shrine dedicated to the pagan god Woden stood. Calling on all who could hear to follow him, Coifi swung his axe through the door of the shrine, and when there was no awful retribution in reply, he smashed all the idols inside and put the place to the torch, burning it to the ground.

It was a supreme act of faith by one who had lived his whole life in fear of these pagan images, and it sent a powerful message throughout the North that the Christian God now reigned.

A few days later Edwin was christened in the small wooden church in York, where the Minster now stands.

On the mound at Goodmanham, where the pagan shrine stood, now stands a Norman church, a shining landmark in the great story of England.

Boynton

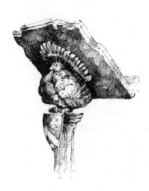

Talking Turkey

ST ANDREW'S CHURCH, BOYNTON, stands at the gates of Boynton Hall, ancestral home of the Strickland family. The main body of the church was restored by John Carr of York after a fire in the 18th century, and the interior is filled with green painted box pews, watched over from the west end by the Strickland family pew, situated on a balcony reached by a grand curving staircase. The attention is immediately drawn to the lectern, which rests on the outspread tail of a turkey – THE ONLY LECTERN IN THE WORLD ADORNED WITH A TURKEY.

St Andrews would be a grand church to attend at Christmas, for turkeys are everywhere, being part of the Strickland family crest. In 1497 the first William Strickland of Boynton travelled to America in the good ship *Matthew* with the Cabot brothers, looking for gold, and later claimed that he was THE FIRST ENGLISHMAN TO SET FOOT IN THE NEW WORLD. He didn't find gold, but he did find turkeys, and brought some back with him, becoming THE MAN WHO INTRODUCED THE TURKEY INTO BRITAIN. William Strickland was the Bernard Matthews of his day and became rich thanks to the turkey, so when he applied for a coat of arms he requested that 'a turkey cock in his pride proper' be incorporated into the design. The crude drawing he made to illustrate the bird, which can still be seen at the College of Arms in London, is THE FIRST KNOWN DRAWING OF A TURKEY.

a height of 5 ft 9 ins (1.75 m).

For a number of years William made appearances at fairs all over England, calling himself the YORKSHIRE GIANT, and charging people a shilling to shake his hand. When he granted an audience to George III, the King gave him a gold watch on a chain, which Bradley wore for the rest of his life.

William Bradley died in Market Weighton, aged just 33, and was buried in All Saints Church – inside to deter grave robbers. There is a memorial to him on the church wall. His house, which was built with especially high ceilings and doorways, is now a shop, and on the wall is a plaque showing his footprint, 15 ins (38 cm) in length and nearly 6 ins (15 cm) wide.

Every May since 1996, Market Weighton has celebrated Giant Bradley Day with stalls, entertainers and exhibitions.

Market Weighton

The Yorkshire Giant

It seems fitting that THE TALLEST-EVER ENGLISHMAN belongs to England's largest county. WILLIAM BRADLEY (1787–1820) was born in the old-fashioned market town of MARKET WEIGHTON, one of 13 children. He weighed 14 lbs (6.35 kg) at birth, and reached his full height of 7 ft 9 ins (2.36 m) by the age of 20, weighing in by then at 27 stone (171 kg). His father, a tailor, only managed to attain

The Kiplingcotes Derby

Oldest Horse Race in the World

'A horse race to be observed and ridd yearly on the third Thursday in March; open to horses of all ages, to convey horsemen's weight, ten stones, exclusive of saddle, to enter ye post before eleven o'clock on the morning of ye race. The race to be run before two.'

In 1618, almost 100 years after it was first run in 1519, they finally got around to drawing up the rules for the KIPLINGCOTES DERBY, THE OLDEST HORSE RACE IN THE WORLD. It began as a way for the local gentry to try out their horses after the winter, hence the March running date. The race begins at noon, when a local villager waves a flag by the ancient stone starting post set in the grass near the old Kiplingcotes railway station. The course follows the route of a Roman road across the Wolds to finish at Londesborough Wold Farm, a distance of 4 miles (6.4 km). These days the winner receives £50, while the runner-up pockets all the entry fees, which, at £4.25 each, can add up to more than the first prize!

The Hudson Way

Kiplingcotes railway station was a stop on the line that ran from York to Beverley, and was put there in 1864 for the convenience of Lord Hotham, who lived at Dalton Hall nearby. The railway line was built by George Hudson, the Railway King, who lived

The Railway King

GEORGE HUDSON, THE RAILWAY KING, (1800–71) was born at Howsham, near Malton. He made a fortune as a draper in York, to which was added a rather dubious legacy from a great-uncle, and he invested it in the railways, persuading George Stephenson to run his railway from Newcastle to London through York rather than Leeds. This was a time of rapid railway expansion, and Hudson's rail empire grew quickly. By 1844 he owned over 1,000 miles of railway, a quarter of all the railways in England, including what became the Midland Railway. He also possessed a string of country estates, including Londesborough. Hudson's downfall came in 1848 when he was accused of using crooked business practices, including the bribing of MPs, and he was bankrupted and forced to flee the country. Even his waxwork at Madame Tussauds was melted down. Hudson eventually died in London, almost broke, and was buried at Scrayingham, not far from where he was born in Yorkshire.

at Londesborough Hall, and also had the use of his own private station at Shiptonthorpe, near his home. The line was closed in 1965, a victim of the Beeching cuts, and a footpath called the Hudson Way now follows the route from Market Weighton to Beverley.

Burton Agnes

The Screaming Skull

BURTON AGNES was named after a daughter of Roger de Stuteville, who built a manor house on the site in 1173. The glorious Norman undercroft from this house still survives and is in the care of English Heritage.

Simon Jenkins described the present Burton Agnes Hall, built of rosy pink brick and stone in the last days of Tudor England, as 'THE PERFECT ENGLISH HOUSE'. Certainly Anne Griffith, youngest daughter of Sir Henry Griffith, builder of the Hall, thought it the most beautiful house she had ever seen.

One afternoon Anne went to visit her friends, the St Quintins, at the nearby village of Harpham, but was attacked and badly beaten by robbers on the way. She was carried back to Burton Agnes and died a few days later. Her last wish was that her head should be severed from her body and preserved in her beloved Burton Agnes for ever, but her sisters defied the macabre request, and Anne was buried in the churchyard next door. From that moment on the family was haunted day and night by ghostly happenings, and eventually they had Anne's grave reopened – to find that her body was perfectly preserved, but

her head was a mere skull. They finally took the skull into the house and the disturbances stopped. From time to time attempts have been made to remove the 'screaming skull' as it became known, but on each occasion there were terrifying noises and pandemonium was unleashed. Finally Anne's head was secretly bricked up in a wall somewhere in the house, no one knows where, and all has remained peaceful ever since.

Harpham

Well, Well

HARPHAM, where Anne was attacked, was the birthplace of ST JOHN OF BEVERLEY (*see* Beverley) and there is a well there called ST JOHN'S WELL, which is said to have healing properties, especially for wild animals. In spring children gather primroses to garland the well, keeping some to take to Beverley Minster to put on St John's tomb.

Not far away is a second, more sinister well, known as the DRUMMER BOY'S WELL. One story says that William the Conqueror promised the lands of Harpham to the first person from his army who reached the village. A drummer boy got there first but was closely pursued by a St Quintin, who did away with the boy, threw his body down the well and then claimed the lands for himself. Another story says that the drummer boy was knocked into the well by accident during an archery tournament. Whichever tale is true, the St Quintins became the local landowners, and whenever a St Quintin is about to die a ghostly drumming can be heard emanating from deep inside the well . . .

Well, I never knew this
about

THE YORKSHIRE WOLDS

The YORKSHIRE WOLDS form THE NORTHERNMOST OUTCROP OF CHALK HILLS IN ENGLAND.

Every July, DRIFFIELD, known as THE CAPITAL OF THE WOLDS, holds THE LARGEST ONE-DAY AGRICULTURAL SHOW IN ENGLAND.

Looming beside the Norman church in RUDSTON, an ancient village on the Roman road from Bridlington to York, is THE TALLEST STANDING STONE IN BRITAIN. It stands over 25 ft (7.6 m) high, and the same length again is buried beneath the surface. No one knows how it got there – the nearest

similar rock formations are at Cayton Bay, 10 miles (16 km) to the north, but it was almost certainly used for religious purposes.

Buried in the churchyard at Rudston, near where she was born, is the author WINIFRED HOLTBY (1898–1935), best known for her novel *South Riding*. Between 1967 and 2002 the Royal Society of Literature awarded the Winifred Holtby Memorial Prize for the best regional novel of the year.

A white cross in the pretty church-yard of NUNBURNHOLME marks the grave of bird lover and conservation-ist FRANCIS ORPEN MORRIS (1810–93), who became Rector there in 1854. He wrote a much-admired *History of British Birds*, first published in 1850, complete with beautiful colour plates, and was one of those responsible for the founding of the ROYAL SOCIETY FOR THE PROTECTION OF BIRDS (RSPB). Between 1866 and his death in 1893 he put together a volume of views of country houses, with 240 woodblocks printed in colour, called *A Series of Picturesque Views of Seats of the Noblemen and Gentlemen of Great Britain and Ireland* or, for short, *Morris's Seats.* This work is now hugely valuable as one of the few picture records of a large number of country houses that have since disappeared.

On the village green at NORTH NEWBALD is a large flat stone known as the WHIPPING STONE, where a man is said to have been whipped to death in 1624, in possibly THE LAST PUBLIC FLOGGING IN ENGLAND.

The church at North Newbald, which lies in a dip in the Wolds, is THE MOST COMPLETE NORMAN CHURCH IN YORKSHIRE, and possibly unique in possessing four superb Norman doorways, one in each wall. Almost unchanged since it was built in 1125, the church has a long, lofty nave with four rich Norman arches supporting the tower. The original Saxon church here was built from locally quarried Newbald stone, which can be found in many of the

older and more splendid churches of the East Riding including Bridlington Priory and Beverley Minster.

The village of ROWLEY is no more. All that is left is the lonely, bewildered Norman church, where the villagers used to get christened, married and buried. Still there are Sir Ralph Ellerker and his three sons, laid to rest at Rowley after dying as heroes at the Battle of Flodden in 1513. Not much more than 100 years later, in 1638, every single one of the villagers of Rowley abandoned their church, their homes and their friends to seek a new life in the New World, free from the religious persecution of King Charles I. Led by their Puritan Nonconformist rector the Revd Ezekiel Rogers, they boarded the ship *John of London* at Hull and embarked on the dangerous journey across the Atlantic to found a new community in Massachusetts, which they called Rowley after the Yorkshire village they had left behind. Their venture is

commemorated in the church by a window which shows Rogers and the families that left Yorkshire for ever. The chalice from which they once drank, dated 1634, remains in the possession of Rowley Church.

The EAST RIDING'S HIGHEST SPIRE, over 200 ft (61 m) tall and a prominent landmark for miles around, can be found in SOUTH DALTON, where it soars above St Mary's Church. St Mary's stands at the gates of Dalton Hall, home of Lord Hotham, for whom the church was designed in 1861 by J.L. Pearson. There are many splendid Hotham tombs inside, transferred from the original brick church.

THIXENDALE is the EAST RIDING'S MOST ISOLATED VILLAGE and until 1997 was unable to receive a television signal. It lies not far from YORKSHIRE'S BEST-PRESERVED DESERTED VILLAGE, WHARRAM PERCY, which was abandoned in the 16th century when the residents were removed to make way for sheep.

The font of St Nicholas, NORTH GRIMSTON, is one of a group of four matchless Norman fonts that can all be found within 10 miles (16 km) of each other in the Yorkshire Wolds. It IS THE ONLY FONT IN BRITAIN TO BOAST A CARVED ILLUSTRATION OF THE DESCENT FROM THE CROSS.

Another of the fonts is in COWLAM church, which is hidden away in the middle of a muddy farmyard. This font is ONE OF ONLY TWO FONTS IN

ENGLAND TO SHOW A REPRESENTA-
TION OF THE MASSACRE OF THE
INNOCENTS.

A third font can be found in ST
MARY'S CHURCH at KIRKBURN, a
spectacular Norman church with a
wonderfully deep entrance doorway,
a magnificent zigzag chancel arch and
a unique stone staircase at the west
end, which climbs steeply up two of
the inside walls and then merges into
a lovely spiral stair.

The fourth font, now in the church
at Langtoft, was saved from the tiny
ruined church at COTTAM, another of
Yorkshire's deserted villages, deci-
mated by the Black Death in the 14th
century.

VALE OF YORK

All Saints, Pocklington, where the 'Flying Man' fell to earth

Pocklington

Of Witches and Bat Wings

POCKLINGTON, a happy, hospitable little market town that sits in the VALE OF YORK at the edge of the Wolds, wasn't always so friendly. In 1630 a mob of enraged townsfolk dragged OLD WIFE GREEN into the market-place and burned her at the stake – making Pocklington almost certainly THE LAST TOWN IN ENGLAND TO BURN A WITCH.

On a happier note, William Wilber-force, the anti-slavery campaigner, was inspired in Pocklington – he attended the Grammar School for five years from 1771. His family took their name from the nearby village of WILBER-FOSS, where they had settled in the 12th century. Other distinguished Old Pocklingtonians are the playwright SIR TOM STOPPARD and comedian ADRIAN EDMONDSON.

A tablet on the side of All Saints Church in Pocklington tells of an incident in 1733 when an acrobat called THOMAS PELLING 'was killed by jumping against the Battlement of ye Choir when coming down ye rope from ye steeple'. Known as the 'Flying Man', Pelling used to don 'bat wings' and perform tricks while balanced on a rope, which stretched from one of the pinnacles on the church tower to the Star Inn in the market-place. On 10 April 1733 the rope for some reason slackened and the Flying Man was flung against the battlements and plunged to the ground, dead. He was buried where he fell. Pocklington now holds an annual Flying Man Festival, named in honour of Thomas Pelling, which is a fund-raising event involving, amongst other treats, abseiling down the church tower . . .

Aughton

Newts? Don't Aske

The Norman church at AUGHTON stands aloof from its isolated village, knee deep in the water meadows of the River Derwent, its ancient churchyard walls often washed by flood water. On a buttress of the church tower there is a lively carving of a wriggling newt, or 'aske', as newts are called by the fen folk. High up on the south wall of the tower is carved a shield, flanked by six smaller shields, or quarterings, under which there is an inscription in French which translates as 'Christopher, second son of Robert Aske, chevalier, ought not to forget the year 1536'.

Pilgrimage of Grace

1536 was certainly a big year for Christopher's brother ROBERT ASKE, oldest son of the local laird, Sir Robert Aske. In that year he took charge of a popular Catholic rising that began in York and spread throughout the northern counties, becoming known as the PILGRIMAGE OF GRACE. While the North had a number of economic and political grievances with Henry VIII, the main thrust of the Pilgrimage was against the break from Rome and the Dissolution of the Monasteries being carried out by the ruthless Thomas Cromwell. A leading London lawyer and scion of an old Yorkshire family, Robert Aske was a sound choice to lead the protestors.

Arriving in London at the head of a huge band of rebels, many thousands strong, Aske sought and was granted an audience with the King, who readily promised that the closing of the monasteries would cease and lands already seized would be restored. Satisfied, the rebels broke up and returned home. The King, however, did not keep his word, and when a second uprising broke out under a kinsman of Aske, Sir Francis Bigod of Settrington, it gave Henry the excuse he needed to arrest the ringleaders, including Robert Aske. In 1537

Aske was hanged in chains from a special scaffold erected outside Clifford's Tower in York.

Hemingbrough

Oldest Misericord

The slender spire of HEMINGBROUGH MINSTER beckons to you from miles away across the Vale of York, and it comes as quite a shock when you get there to find that it belongs to a village church and not a cathedral. The exquisite spire is twice the height of the tower on which it rests, soaring to 191 ft (58 m) above the little community at its feet, and such is its height that the church looks as

though it has been squeezed from both ends, causing the spire to shoot upwards – but the effect is still rather splendid.

Carved on the tower mouldings is a row of washing tuns, or tubs, put there as a visual pun on the name of the man who built the tower – Prior Washington (*see* Selby, West Riding).

In 1989 *Blue Peter* presenter CARON KEATING was televised climbing the spire to fix a new weathervane.

The glory of the interior, which is a happy jumble of different styles from Norman to Victorian, are the wood carvings on the screen and the pew ends, which portray a veritable zoo of demons, dragons, dogs and monkeys, as well as a capering jester with cap and bells. In the choir can be found THE OLDEST MISERICORD IN ENGLAND, thought to date from about 1200.

Riccall

Twilight of Saxon England

RICCALL lies on a bend of the River Ouse between York and Selby. The splendid Norman church on the quiet green replaced an earlier Saxon church, which could well have been witness to events that profoundly changed the course of British history.

Battle of Fulford

In September 1066 the Norwegian King HARALD HARDRADA moored his fleet of 300 ships in the shallow River Ouse at Riccall and made camp, having sailed up the Humber in company with TOSTIG, the banished brother of King Harold of England. Their aim was the conquest of England, no less, and their first intention was to capture York to use as a base. However, at FULFORD, now a suburb of York but open fields then, they were confronted by the forces of the Northern Earls, Morcar of Northumbria and Edwin of Mercia, and battle was joined.

The result was a victory for Hardrada. The forces of the Northern English were scattered, and couriers were sent down the coast by boat to inform King Harold, who was in the south with the main English army guarding against the expected arrival of William of Normandy. Harold was forced to race north to deal with this new threat.

Battle of Stamford Bridge

Harold and Hardrada met where the STAMFORD BRIDGE crosses the River Derwent, north-east of York, only five days after the Battle of Fulford. The Norwegian army, weakened by losses suffered at Fulford, was taken completely by surprise by the sheer speed with which the English had marched north to Yorkshire. Harold won an overwhelming victory and Hardrada was slain. Of the 300 ships that had anchored at Riccall only 24 returned to Norway.

For Harold, though, triumph was short-lived. Less than three weeks later, after another forced march back south, his exhausted army were overcome by the Normans at Hastings and Harold lay dead.

The first links in that momentous chain of events that brought Norman rule to England, and eventually to Scotland and Ireland as well, were forged in the quiet water meadows of Yorkshire's East Riding. The bend in the River Ouse at Riccall where the saga began is little changed, still as empty and atmospheric as it must have been when the sails of the Norse fleet appeared above the rushes on that fateful September evening in 1066. Less than one month later two kings lay dead and England had a new king – one who would create a completely new England.

There is still a bridge over the Derwent at Stamford Bridge, for this spot remains an important strategic crossing between York and the East Riding, but few realise that they are driving past the scene of THE LAST SAXON VICTORY IN ENGLAND.

Well, I never knew this
about
THE VALE OF YORK

ESCRICK HALL, south of York, was home to SIR THOMAS KNYVET, who led the search party that discovered Guy Fawkes beneath the Houses of Parliament on 5 November 1605.

HOLME UPON SPALDING MOOR was the birthplace of NORTHERN FOODS, one of Britain's largest food companies, founded in 1937 by ALEX HORSLEY under the name Northern Dairies.

The gardens of BURNBY HALL in Pocklington boast THE LARGEST COLLECTION IN EUROPE OF HARDY WATER LILIES IN A NATURAL SETTING.

ALLERTHORPE, near Pocklington, was the birthplace of telescope maker THOMAS COOKE (1807–68), founder of the optical firm T. Cooke & Sons, who opened his first business in Stonegate, near York Minster, in 1837.

His inventiveness and skill, as well as the reliability of his instruments, made Britain the leading manufacturer of telescopes in the world. Not long before he died, Cooke built what was then THE LARGEST REFRACTING TELESCOPE IN THE WORLD, THE NEWALL TELESCOPE, for a rich industrialist called Robert Newall, who had a private observatory near Gateshead in County Durham. On Newall's death the telescope was

donated to Cambridge University, and in 1959 it was moved to the Greek National Observatory in Athens, where it is still in service. There are a number of Thomas Cooke's telescopes that are still in operation, including one in the National Observatory of New Zealand, one in Tasmania, two in Scotland and two in York.

North Riding

HISTORIC CLEVELAND

Middlesborough's Transporter Bridge, the largest in the world

Middlesbrough

'Yarm was, Stockton is,
Middlesbrough will be'
TEESSIDE PROVERB

MIDDLESBROUGH today is a vast, sprawling industrial landscape of belching chimneys and smoke that fills the wide vale below the high Cleveland Hills. It was once a peaceful place of churches and water meadows. The oldest remnant of a settlement in the area is a Norman font from the church of St Hilda, part of a Benedictine priory founded in what is now the centre of Middlesbrough in the 12th century. The font was placed in the new St Hilda's, built in 1840, and when this church was burned down in 1969 the font was taken to the Dorman Museum, where it now lives.

Mydilsburgh was originally the 'middle place' between the great Christian centres of Whitby and Durham. In 1801 it was just a tiny hamlet of four farms and 25 people, but within 150 years it had grown to be BRITAIN'S BIGGEST PRODUCER OF IRON AND STEEL with THE LARGEST PETRO-CHEMICAL CENTRE IN EUROPE.

This extraordinary expansion began in 1830 when a group of Quaker businessmen, led by Joseph Pease, bought some land at Middlesbrough to build a port on the River Tees for shipping out coal from their Durham coalfields. They also extended the Stockton and Darlington railway to bring the coal to the port.

In 1841 JOHN VAUGHAN (1799–1868) and HENRY BOLCKOW (1806–78), who are considered to be the founders of modern Middlesbrough, established MIDDLESBROUGH'S FIRST IRON FOUNDRY, and ten years later built MIDDLESBROUGH'S FIRST BLAST FURNACE to exploit the iron ore newly found in the Cleveland Hills. In 1853 Bolckow became MIDDLESBROUGH'S FIRST MAYOR and later its FIRST MP. In 1863 Bolckow and Vaughan discovered a rich bed of rock salt beneath their ironworks, which they began to extract, thus building the foundations of Middlesbrough's mighty chemical industry.

Industrial Middlesbrough

'This remarkable place, the youngest child of England's enterprise, is an infant, but if an infant, an infant Hercules'
WILLIAM GLADSTONE, 1862

By 1865 Middlesbrough had become THE WORLD'S BIGGEST PRODUCER OF IRON, PRODUCING ONE-THIRD OF BRITAIN'S OUTPUT, much of it used to build railways all over the world. Steel production began in 1879 and Middlesbrough became THE WORLD LEADER IN STEEL PRODUCTION. As the commentator Sir H.G. Reid put it, 'The iron of Eston . . . has crept out of the Cleveland Hills where it has slept since Roman days and now, like a strong and invincible serpent, coils itself around the world.'

Building Bridges

Middlesbrough gained a particular reputation for building bridges, with DORMAN LONG, founded in 1875, being perhaps the greatest of the bridge manufacturers. Dorman Long made bridges to span the Bosporus, the Nile, the Yangtze, the Thames at Lambeth and the Zambezi at Victoria Falls. Two iconic bridges that proudly bear the stamp 'Made in Middlesbrough are the TYNE

BRIDGE in Newcastle (1928) and the SYDNEY HARBOUR BRIDGE in Australia (1932).

The TEES NEWPORT BRIDGE in Middlesbrough, built by Dorman Long and opened in 1934, was THE FIRST VERTICAL LIFT BRIDGE IN BRITAIN and is THE HEAVIEST IN THE WORLD. The central lifting span is 270 ft (82.3m) wide and rises to leave a clear headway of 120 ft (36.6 m) above high water. At its peak in the 1940s the bridge was raised 300 times a year, but owing to declining river traffic, in 1990 it was raised for the last time and then sealed in the down position to serve as a conventional road bridge.

The most famous symbol of Middlesbrough today is THE WORLD'S LARGEST TRANSPORTER BRIDGE, built by Sir William Arrol & Co, builders of the Forth Railway Bridge in Scotland, and opened in 1911. It is ONE OF ONLY TWO TRANSPORTER BRIDGES IN BRITAIN (the other is in Newport, South Wales) and spans the River Tees, linking Middlesbrough with Port Clarence on the north bank. In what is one of Yorkshire's most fascinating jaunts you walk or drive on to

a waiting gondola, which is suspended from the bridge's main crossbeam, and are then carried high across the river for an exhilarating ride of 571 ft (174 m) that takes some 90 seconds. The gondola is designed to carry 860 people or up to nine vehicles and their occupants.

In 1974, in the dark, TV comic actor TERRY SCOTT drove his car off the bridge approach on the Port Clarence side, thinking he had come to a fixed bridge. His car was saved from falling into the river by the safety netting.

Middlesbrough Steel

Middlesbrough steel can also be found in Britain's tallest building, Canary Wharf in London, and in the arch of the new Wembley Stadium.

In common with the rest of Britain, steel production in Middlesbrough has been in decline since the 1970s, and in 2009 the Redcar steelworks, which has THE BIGGEST BLAST FURNACE IN EUROPE, was mothballed, perhaps presaging the end of 150 years of steelmaking in Middlesbrough.

Middlesbrough Architecture

Being almost entirely a Victorian creation, Middlesbrough is not renowned for its beautiful architecture – especially as much of the city was flattened when it became the first industrial centre to be bombed in the Second World War. There are two Grade I listed houses of note, however, both of which lie to the south of the city centre.

ACKLAM HALL was built in 1680 for Sir William Hustler, and remained in the Hustler family until 1928, when it was sold to Middlesbrough Corporation and used as a school. Middlesbrough College vacated the building in 2009 and the future of the Hall is uncertain.

ORMESBY HALL was built in rather severe Palladian style by the Penny-man family in the 1740s, and the family lived there until 1983, although they handed it over to the National Trust in 1961. It stands in a quiet park on the edge of Middlesbrough and is a welcome haven from the noise and smoke of the city. The interior of the house is noted for its fine plaster-work and wood carvings, while the lavish stables were designed by John Carr of York and are now rented out to the Cleveland Mounted Police.

Acklam Hall

Ormesby possesses THE ONLY MODEL RAILWAY ON PERMANENT DISPLAY AT A NATIONAL TRUST PROPERTY.

Yarm

Cradle of the Railways

For the Old Norse, YARM was 'a place to catch fish', and that is how it features in the Domesday Book in 1086. It was also the highest crossing point on the tidal river, which is why a town was founded here by the de Brus family, ancestors of Robert the Bruce, in the 12th century. This soon developed into Teesside's principal port, and remained so until displaced by Stockton in the 18th century.

Today, Yarm has settled into being a picturesque, yet surprisingly busy, market town. The spacious old town centre fits into a loop of the river and consists of one long main street with wide, cobbled verges and rows of old inns and Georgian houses. Narrow 'wynds', lined with cottages and tiny gardens, lead away from the market place and down to the river. The whole effect is delightful.

In the middle of it all stands the red-brick town hall of 1710, now made useful as a rather charming public lavatory. High up on the walls of the town hall are various flood marks – indeed, these can be found on buildings all around the town, signifying that Yarm was regularly flooded, with the market more than once under 4 ft (1.2 m) of water.

Birth of the Railway

Also on one wall of the town hall is a plaque showing a picture of Locomotion Number 1, with underneath the names of five men, Thomas Meynell (President), Benjamin Flounders, Jeremiah Cairns, Richard Miles and Thomas Miles. On 12 February 1820 these five men gathered at the nearby George and Dragon Inn for a meeting that would have far-reaching consequences. They were there to promote the idea of building a railway from Stockton to Darlington – a railway that would open five years later in 1825 and be THE VERY FIRST PUBLIC RAILWAY IN THE WORLD. That day, quiet, unobtrusive Yarm, a place to catch fish, gave birth to a revolution that changed the world.

It is quite difficult to forget the railways when you are in Yarm, for rearing high above the rooftops, dwarfing the houses beneath it, is one of the biggest viaducts in Britain, 2,280 ft (695 m) long with 43 arches. It strides through the heart of the town like a colossus before crossing the river just upstream of the Bishop of Durham's stone road bridge of 1400.

Last Knight Banneret

One of Yarm's little cottages once belonged to a genuine 18th-century hero, Tom Brown (1705–46), a Hussar who fought at the Battle of Dettingen in 1743 and rode into the thick of the action to rescue the Regimental Standard.

'He had two horses killed from under him; two fingers of ye bridal hand chopped off; and after retaking the standard from ye Gen D'Arms, whom he killed, he made his way through a lane of the enemy, exposed to fire and sword, in the execution of which he received 8 cuts in ye face, head and neck; 2 balls lodged in his back, 3 went thro his hat; and in this hack'd condition he rejoined his regiment who gave him three huzzas on his arrival.'

For his bravery Tom Brown became THE LAST MAN EVER TO BE MADE A KNIGHT BANNERET BY A BRITISH MONARCH ON THE BATTLEFIELD – in

A KNIGHT BANNERET was a knight who had distinguished himself in battle and was thereafter entitled by the King to carry his own small banner or banneret. He could raise a body of officers and men to serve under his banner and they would be paid for by the King. A Knight Banneret could only be knighted actually on the battlefield, and since Dettingen was the last battle at which a British monarch personally led his troops into battle, it was also the last time a Knight Banneret was so created.

this case George II. Tom used his reward money to buy his cottage in Yarm and ran it as an inn. He died there, still full of bullets, and is buried in the parish churchyard.

Kirkleatham

A Hospital and a Hall

KIRKLEATHAM is a handsome conservation village hidden by trees from the industrial squalor that surrounds it. Actually, it is scarcely a village, more of a collection of extraordinary

buildings, the most astonishing of which is the hospital, probably the loveliest almshouse in England. It was built in 1676 by the local squire, SIR WILLIAM TURNER, the Lord Mayor of London who organised the rebuilding of the city after the Great Fire. At the heart of the U-shaped range of buildings is a glorious chapel designed by James Gibb, which opened in 1742 and is UNIQUE IN THE NORTH OF ENGLAND. The hospital, which was designed to house '10 aged ladies, 10 aged men, 10 young orphan girls and 10 young orphan boys', still provides shelter for about 30 elderly people.

Opposite the ornamental wrought-iron gates of the hospital is a driveway leading to the impressive Queen Anne KIRKLEATHAM OLD HALL, opened in 1709 as a free school. For a while in the 19th century it was a private house; troops were billeted there in the Great War, and now it provides a very grand home for the local museum.

In the grounds of the Old Hall is

Kirkleatham Old Hall

an OWL CENTRE which is home to THE LARGEST COLLECTION OF OWLS IN BRITAIN, as well as hawks, falcons, vultures and even some kookaburras. There are flying demonstrations, and visitors are allowed to get close to the birds – it is a most fascinating place.

Guisborough

de Brus

GUISBOROUGH PRIORY was founded in 1119 by Robert de Brus, ancestor of Robert the Bruce (Robert I) of Scotland, and became one of the richest priories in the North. Buried there in 1295 was King Robert's grandfather, Robert Bruce the Competitor, who was denied the Scottish throne by Edward I when the English king nominated John Balliol instead. The magnificent Bruce Cenotaph, carved with representations of prominent Scottish and English Bruces, which was presented to the priory by Henry VII's daughter Margaret, was moved into the nearby church of St Nicholas at the Dissolution of the Monasteries, and can still be seen there.

Little remains of the priory except the distinctive east gable, which stands nearly 100 ft (30 m) high and acts as a symbol of Guisborough.

Birth of the Chemical Industry

Stone from the ruined priory was used to build the Elizabethan GISBOROUGH HALL, now a hotel, then the home of SIR THOMAS CHALONER (1561–1615), who could be said to be THE FOUNDER OF BRITAIN'S CHEMICAL INDUSTRY. In 1580 Sir Thomas, a statesman with an interest in natural history, travelled to Italy and was shown around the Pope's alum works at Puteoli. Noticing that the surrounding vegetation and conditions were similar to those of his own land at Guisborough, he returned home and opened his own mines – THE FIRST ALUM MINES IN ENGLAND. The mines were run with the help of some of the Pope's own workers, who were smuggled into England hidden in casks, an outrage for which Sir Thomas was excommunicated.

Chaloner's alum mines quickly grew very profitable, alum then being used for dying wool, and wool being England's most important industry. Previously alum had to be imported from the Papal States, which was expensive and unreliable – indeed, when Henry VIII was excommunicated imports were stopped altogether. Chaloner's mines were so successful that they were eventually purloined by Charles I for himself – hardly surprising then that Chaloner's son

Thomas was one of those only too happy to sign the King's death warrant in 1649.

Captain Cook

(1728–79)

Birthplace

The village of MARTON, now part of Middlesbrough, was the birthplace in 1728 of explorer JAMES COOK, the son of a farm worker. The cottage where he was born was demolished in 1786 to make way for a mansion house, itself later destroyed by fire, and the site, which is now a park, is marked by a large urn. Nearby, housed in a modern building, is the CAPTAIN COOK BIRTHPLACE MUSEUM, opened in 1978.

On display inside the rebuilt parish church of St Cuthbert is the register containing this entry: 'James the son of James Cook day labourer baptized'. A piece of Norman carving from the original church building now has pride of place in the church at

Gisborne in New Zealand, near where Cook first stepped ashore on New Zealand in 1769.

On the village green there is a stone memorial brought from Point Hicks, the first place in Australia sighted by Cook in 1770.

Schooldays

When Cook was eight years old his family moved 6 miles (9.6 km) down the road to AIREYHOLME FARM in GREAT AYTON, a large village on the River Leven, where his father got a job as a farm bailiff, working for the Lord of the Manor Thomas Scottowe. Obviously impressed with the young Cook, Scottowe paid for him to attend the local Postgate School, where Cook showed the aptitude for mathematics that he would later apply to the art of navigation. It is said that he never once got his sums wrong. The school is now the CAPTAIN COOK SCHOOLROOM MUSEUM and contains a reconstruction of an 18th-century schoolroom.

Captain Cook's Cottage

In 1755, the year that James Cook joined the Royal Navy, his father moved the rest of the family into a stone cottage in Great Ayton that he had built himself, carving his initials and those of his wife above the front door. In 1933 this cottage was sold and

shipped to Australia, where it was re-erected in Fitzroy Park in Melbourne, Victoria, to commemorate the state's centennial. Every brick, stone and timber was numbered and catalogued so that the cottage could be rebuilt as faithfully as possible, using the original nails, and with the walls constructed to the same degree of crookedness as in Yorkshire. In its place in Great Ayton is a granite obelisk hewn from rocks near Point Hicks (*see* above).

An even bigger obelisk in memory of Captain Cook stands high above the town on Easby Moor.

They Rest in Peace

In the churchyard of All Saints, where Cook's family worshipped, are the graves of his mother and five of his brothers and sisters, four of whom died before they were five years old.

Captain Cook's father, who died in 1779 without knowing that his son had been killed two months earlier in Hawaii, is buried in the churchyard of St Germains in Marske on the coast.

Grocer's Boy

In 1745, when he was 16, Cook got a job in William Sanderson's grocery in the historic fishing (and smuggling) port of STAITHES. Here, like so many who come today, he was seduced by the lure of the sea, and soon fretted in the confines of the shop, proving to be not much good as a grocer's boy. One morning in 1746, not 18 months after he had arrived, James Cook gathered up his belongings and walked out of the door to make his way across the moors to his date with destiny in Whitby.

The shop where he worked was lost to the sea in 1812, but some of its materials were saved and used in a new building that now houses the CAPTAIN COOK & STAITHES HERITAGE CENTRE.

Apprentice

Arriving in WHITBY, Cook went to stay with John and Henry Walker, two prominent Quaker ship-owners he had been introduced to by his previous employer William Sanderson. They offered him an apprenticeship, and for three years he sailed the east coast on a number of Whitby 'cats', small sturdy vessels used mainly for

coastal work. All four ships in which Cook later sailed on his epic explorations were built in Whitby. In fact, HM Bark *Endeavour*, in which Cook made his first voyage of discovery in 1768–71, was a converted Whitby cat.

The house in Grape Lane where Cook lived (in the attic) survives today as the CAPTAIN COOK MEMORIAL MUSEUM, and there is a bronze statue of him looking out to sea on the west cliff in Whitby.

Achievements

- 1759 Surveyed and mapped the entrance to the St Lawrence Seaway, enabling General Wolfe to carry out his surprise attack on Quebec across the Plains of Abraham.
- 1763–7 Surveyed and produced THE FIRST ACCURATE MAPS OF NEWFOUNDLAND.
- 1769 Became THE FIRST EUROPEAN TO CIRCUMNAVIGATE AND MAP NEW ZEALAND. The first place sighted in

New Zealand was a chalk headland that Cook named Young Nick's Head after the ship's boy who spotted it.

- 1770 Became THE FIRST EUROPEAN TO EXPLORE THE EAST COAST OF AUSTRALIA, which he named New South Wales and claimed for Britain. The first place he sighted he called Point Hicks after the lieutenant who had first spotted land. His first landfall was at Botany Bay, near where Sydney is now, in April 1770.

- 1773 Became THE FIRST MAN TO CROSS THE ANTARCTIC CIRCLE.

- 1778 Became THE FIRST EUROPEAN TO SEE THE HAWAIIAN ISLANDS. He named them the Sandwich Islands in honour of the First Lord of the Admiralty, the Earl of Sandwich – inventor of the sandwich.

- 1778–9 Surveyed and produced THE FIRST ACCURATE CHARTS OF THE COASTLINE OF THE AMERICAN NORTH WEST, from California to Alaska.

Forever England . . .

James Cook died in 1779, on a beach in Hawaii at the hands of natives. The spot where he died is today marked by an obelisk, erected in 1874. A small patch of land around it was bought for Britain by the British consul general, and has forever since been maintained by the Royal Navy.

Well, I never knew this about

HISTORIC CLEVELAND

Although it sounds like a pudding, ROSEBERRY TOPPING is in fact a cone-shaped height that overlooks Teesside. At 1,049 ft (320 m) it may not be the highest but is certainly the most distinctive peak on the North Yorkshire Moors. A young James Cook, already eager to explore, would regularly scramble to the top from his home in Great Ayton, and gaze longingly out to sea.

Roseberry Topping gave a title to a distinguished Scottish family, one of whom, the 5th Earl of Rosebery, became Prime Minister in 1894. The wife of the 1st Earl was a Yorkshire lass, whose family home was within sight of the mountain.

AGNES SPENCER, wife of Thomas Spencer, co-founder of Marks & Spencer, was born in MARTON, and is buried in the parish churchyard there.

STOKESLEY, famous for its old pack-horse bridge, was the birthplace in 1817 of JANE PACE, THE FIRST WHITE WOMAN TO LIVE IN THE STATE OF VICTORIA, AUSTRALIA. She settled in Portland Bay with her husband, Stephen Henty, in 1836.

REDCAR is home to THE OLDEST SURVIVING LIFEBOAT IN THE WORLD, THE ZETLAND, which is displayed in a dedicated museum on the Esplanade. Built in 1800 and named after local landowner the Marquess of Zetland, she served Redcar for 78 years and saved over 500 lives.

CLEVELAND GOLF CLUB at Redcar was THE FIRST GOLF CLUB FORMED IN YORKSHIRE, and is THE ONLY TRUE LINKS COURSE IN YORKSHIRE.

Redcar racecourse is one of the few racecourses in England to possess a straight mile.

The Cliff Lift at SALTBURN is THE OLDEST WATER-BALANCED CLIFF LIFT IN BRITAIN. It opened in 1884.

MARSKE HALL, built in 1625, was the home of the Marquesses of Zetland from 1762 until 1943. It is now a Cheshire Home.

In 1905 MIDDLESBROUGH FOOTBALL CLUB paid THE FIRST-EVER FOUR-FIGURE TRANSFER FEE when they bought ALF COMMON from Sunderland for £1,000.

The beautifully situated 17th-century church at UPLEATHAM, which measures 18 ft (5.5 m) by 15 ft (4.6 m), is a contender for the title of BRITAIN'S SMALLEST CHURCH.

BOB CHAMPION, the jockey who won the Grand National in 1981 two years after being diagnosed with cancer, was born in GUISBOROUGH in 1948. ALDANITI, the horse he rode to victory, was recovering from a life-threatening injury himself. In 1983 their story was made into a film called *Champions*, in which Bob Champion was played by John Hurt.

CHARLES LUTWIDGE DODGSON, better known as Lewis Carroll, lived from the age of 11 in the Elizabethan Rectory at CROFT, where his father was Rector from 1843 to 1868. Emma Pickersgill, who died in 1933 at the age of 90, remembered the theatrical games and puppet shows full of strange characters that young Dodgson used to stage in the Rectory garden. Apparently, he loved her griddlecakes and would frequently call round to her home, Lilac Cottage, to enjoy some with a cup of tea.

LORD BYRON and his unhappy new wife spent their three-week honeymoon at HANLABY HALL in 1815 and attended St Peter's Church in Croft. Apparently George Hudson, the Railway King, also attended church at St Peter's and when bored with the sermon would turn his back on the Rector, while his wife Elizabeth would put up her parasol.

YARM'S METHODIST CHAPEL was built in 1763 and is THE OLDEST OCTAGONAL METHODIST CHAPEL IN THE WORLD STILL IN USE BY METHODISM.

Set on top of a garden wall opposite the church in Yarm is a rather unusual curiosity – a little tableau consisting of a tiny castle with a keep and bastion towers, and beside it a model of Yarm town hall. It was put there 100 years ago, but no one knows why or by whom.

THE CLEVELAND BAY, bred in the 17th century by uniting the Chapman packhorses of Yorkshire's many monasteries with the North African 'Barb' or Arabian horses imported into Whitby, is Britain's oldest breed of horse. Cleveland Bays are used to draw the Queen's carriages.

NORTH RIDING COAST

The Rotunda, the world's first dedicated museum of geology

Scarborough

First Resort

The view from Scarborough's castle, standing 300 ft (90 m) above the sea, is truly spectacular – golden beaches curving away to jagged cliff headlands north and south, smart white terraces basking in the sun, the jumbled red roofs of the old town tumbling down towards a little harbour filled with pleasure yachts and fishing boats.

SCARBOROUGH is the largest of Yorkshire's coastal towns, and for a long while has been a town of many faces. For 500 years from 1253 until the middle of the 18th century, Scarborough held ONE OF THE LARGEST TRADING FAIRS IN EUROPE, attended by merchants from all over the Continent, and commemorated in song by Simon and Garfunkel:

'Are you going to Scarborough Fair?
Parsley, sage, rosemary and thyme . . . '

Scarborough's Town Hall occupies a Tudor mansion that was once the home of the Harland family, one of whom, SIR EDWARD JAMES HARLAND (1831–1905), founded the great Belfast shipyard of Harland and Wolff, where the *Titanic* was constructed.

Scarborough was THE FIRST ENGLISH SEASIDE RESORT. In 1626 Elizabeth Farrow discovered a spring at the base of a cliff on the south beach, which she believed had health-giving properties. Her claim was confirmed in 1660 when a Dr Wittie wrote a book about the medical benefits of the fine spa waters of Scarborough, and this attracted people with ailments from all across Yorkshire and beyond.

THE FIRST BATHING MACHINES IN ENGLAND were introduced in Scarborough in 1735, and in 1845 visitors were welcomed into one of England's FIRST PURPOSE-BUILT HOTELS, THE CROWN, overlooking the South Bay.

Round

In 1829 THE WORLD'S FIRST DEDICATED MUSEUM OF GEOLOGY, THE ROTUNDA, only THE SECOND PURPOSE-BUILT MUSEUM IN BRITAIN, was opened in Scarborough to showcase the work of WILLIAM SMITH, known as the 'Father of Geology'. Smith produced THE FIRST GEOLOGICAL MAP OF BRITAIN (a copy of which is on display in the museum), and came to Scarborough to examine the geologically rich and fossil-laden Yorkshire coastline.

William Smith suggested both the innovative round shape of the building and the design of the displays inside, which remain almost unchanged to this day. Likewise,

the original glass display cabinets installed in 1830 are still in place, having been restored, and they create a wonderfully evocative and instructive experience.

Grand

On 25 May 1849, the writer ANNE BRONTË, racked with consumption, came to Scarborough with her sister Charlotte, in the hope that the fresh sea air might help her to recover, but she was already too weak, and died three days later. True to Charlotte's desire to 'lay the flower where it had fallen', Anne is buried in the churchyard of St Mary's, high above the bay, in the shadow of the castle. A blue plaque outside Scarborough's huge Grand Hotel marks the site of Wood's Lodgings, where Anne died.

When it opened in 1867 the GRAND HOTEL was THE LARGEST PURPOSE-BUILT HOTEL IN EUROPE, and one of THE LARGEST BRICK BUILDINGS IN THE WORLD. It has a distinctive 'V' shape and was designed around the theme of 'Time', with 365 bedrooms, 52

chimneys, 12 floors and 4 towers.

In 1914 the top two floors had to be demolished because of the severe damage caused when Scarborough became THE FIRST TOWN IN ENGLAND TO BE FIRED UPON BY THE GERMANS IN THE FIRST WORLD WAR, bombarded from offshore by two cruisers of the German High Fleet.

Round Again

In 1955 Stephen Joseph established BRITAIN'S FIRST THEATRE-IN-THE-ROUND in Scarborough. It is now run by SIR ALAN AYCKBOURN, said to be THE MOST PERFORMED LIVING PLAYWRIGHT IN THE WORLD, who has premiered the majority of his 73 plays in Scarborough.

BORN IN SCARBOROUGH

LORD LEIGHTON (1830–96), sculptor and artist, was born at 13 Brunswick Terrace. President of the Royal Academy from 1878 until his death, he was THE FIRST ARTIST TO BE MADE A PEER, an honour he received on the day before he died.

CHARLES LAUGHTON (1899–1962), actor. In 1934 he became THE FIRST ENGLISH ACTOR TO BE AWARDED AN OSCAR when he was voted Best Actor for his performance in the title role in *The Private Life of Henry VIII.*

SIR BEN KINGSLEY, actor, was born Krishna Bhanji in the village of Snainton, near Scarborough, in 1943. He won the Oscar for Best Actor in 1982 for his portrayal of Mahatma Gandhi in Richard Attenborough's film *Gandhi.*

ANDY HORNBY, born 1967. He was CEO of the Halifax Bank of Scotland (HBOS) until the bank's forced merger with Lloyds TSB during the banking crisis of 2008.

Brompton

The Birthplace of Aviation

BROMPTON is a rambling village that falls away into the vale on the road from Scarborough to Pickering. The mainly 14th-century All Saints church has a noble buttressed tower with broached spire and stands high on a bank overlooking its charge.

A Poet's Marriage

It was a proud moment for Brompton when, on a golden red autumn day in 1802, the poet WILLIAM WORDSWORTH came here to be married to a local girl, MARY HUTCHINSON, his childhood friend and 'a perfect woman, nobly planned . . . with something of angelic light'.

First in Flight

But then Brompton has much to be proud of, for this quiet, dignified Yorkshire village is also the place where, in 1853, Man's greatest dream came true – MAN LEARNED TO FLY.

A modest little brown brick building beside the main road, unnoticed by the crowds who rush by on their way to the candyfloss and donkey rides of Scarborough, was once the workshop of a man who ranks alongside Newton and da Vinci, whose genius gave us wings and whose endeavours made the world a smaller and more accessible place.

First Flight

SIR GEORGE CAYLEY (1773–1857), Squire of Brompton and descendant of Sire de Cailly, a follower of William the Conqueror, had been mulling over the theory of flight since he was a boy. His observations of gliding seagulls had led him to believe that the idea of flapping wings was not going to

work. Instead, a suitably curved wing, allied to the forward motion of the plane, would create the necessary lift.

So, in 1853, he disappeared into his workshop and set about constructing a glider based on these scientific principles. After a few false starts he emerged, blinking in the light, and towing behind him a monoplane, equipped with kite-shaped cloth wings, an adjustable tailplane and fin, a boat-shaped cockpit for the pilot, and a flimsy tricycle undercarriage. He wheeled the ensemble across the road to the high side of a little valley in the grounds and sat back to ponder his next problem. Who was going to fly the thing?

Naturally he, Sir George, could not. He was 80 years old and his wife, who had never approved of his experiments, especially when he brought them inside the house to try out on the stairs, would not have allowed it.

Fortuitously, at that moment, his coachman JOHN APPLEBY sauntered by, casting an indulgent but rheumy eye over the machine – he had seen many such contraptions before. 'Ah, John,' said Sir George, 'just the chap.'

Before he knew what was happening, Appleby found himself sitting in the tiny cockpit, perched on the edge of the abyss, in front of a spellbound throng of household staff who had gathered, eager to help. They manhandled the glider into position, gave a push and the hapless coachman hurtled off down the slope. The ground fell away and he soared up, up like a bird, into the Yorkshire sky.

For a moment there was a sensation of utter peace and he was floating like an autumn leaf. Then, with dreadful suddenness, the other side of the valley loomed up and, in the words of Sir George's 10-year-old granddaughter, he 'came down with a smash'.

John Appleby, Yorkshireman, had joined the gods – THE FIRST MAN EVER TO FLY AN AEROPLANE. The intrepid fellow extricated himself from the wreckage, brushed himself down, rose to his full height, fixed his excited employer with an accusing eye and spoke as only a Yorkshireman could at such an historic moment: 'Sir George, I wish to give notice. I was hired to drive, not to fly!' And he turned on his heels and limped away into immortality.

Second Flight

In 2003, to mark the 150th anniversary, a modern aviation pioneer, SIR RICHARD BRANSON, recreated John Appleby's flight by flying a replica of Sir George Cayley's flyer across the very same Brompton Dale. Like John Appleby, he was piloting an aeroplane for the first time, but his response was a little more enthusiastic. 'That was exhilarating, magnificent. I can retire knowing that I can fly!'

As a spectacular way of illustrating what Sir George had started in his garden in 1853, there was a flypast by the RAF Red Arrows and by a massive Virgin 747 Jumbo Jet, which flew over the dale at 500 ft (152 m) – an experience that no one who was there will ever forget, and a fitting tribute to the man who taught us all how to fly.

Sir George Cayley can truly be said to have founded the science of aerodynamics, being THE FIRST PERSON TO FORMULATE AND WRITE DOWN THE AERODYNAMICS OF FIXED-WING POWERED FLIGHT, AND THE RELATIONSHIP BETWEEN WEIGHT, LIFT, DRAG AND THRUST. He studied the effects of aerofoils, cambered wings and streamlining, designed an internal combustion engine for aircraft propulsion, WAS THE FIRST TO DESIGN A BIPLANE and THE FIRST TO DESIGN A GLIDER THAT COULD CARRY A MAN, and he pioneered all the basic features of a modern aeroplane.

His legacy was a true understanding of the nature of flight. As he wrote in his notebook, 'When I am gone you may find the seeds of thought in these scrawls.' Fifty years later the Wright Brothers gave due credit to the brilliance of those scrawls when they flew above the sands of Kitty Hawk. North Carolina claims the title 'First in Flight'. Wrong. It was second. Yorkshire was first.

Sir George Cayley's small workshop beside the road in Brompton has been made into a fascinating museum of his life and work, indeed a place of pilgrimage for anyone interested in aviation and this remarkable man.

Re-inventing the Wheel

Although Sir George Cayley is remembered most particularly for that momentous aeroplane flight, it was actually just the crowning achievement of his fertile mind. He even RE-INVENTED THE WHEEL, not once but twice. To provide a light but strong wheel for the undercarriage of his gliders he designed THE TENSION WHEEL WITH SPOKES, as is now used on every modern bicycle. And for

making progress over difficult terrain he invented THE CATERPILLAR TRACK, as used today by tanks and industrial plant – he called it the universal railway.

Staithes

Pronounced 'Steers'

STAITHES is the least known and least spoiled of the many fishing communities along the North Yorkshire coast. One hundred years ago Staithes was one of the most important fishing ports in England. Today, fishing has been replaced by tourism, which is not surprising because the old part of Staithes is like a film set – an archetypal fishing village,

Other Cayley Inventions

THE THEATRE SAFETY CURTAIN, invented after the Covent Garden Theatre had burned down in 1808 and now compulsory in all theatres.

A WORKING ARTIFICIAL HAND, for the son of one of his estate workers who had lost his hand in an accident.

RAILWAY BUFFERS.

hidden in a narrow cleft between enormous red cliffs, and utterly intoxicating.

There is one extremely steep cobbled street that winds down to a tiny harbour, where the seafront, Seaton Garth, is watched over by the Cod and Lobster pub – at least three of the pub's predecessors have been washed away by the waves. Narrow passages and little alleyways snake in and out of cottages and shops, and the breeze is always off the sea.

Art

Artists have long been drawn to Staithes, and when the railway arrived at the end of the 19th century it brought with it the first of a flock of painters, inspired by the Impressionists, who would become known as the STAITHES GROUP. In 1898 LAURA JOHNSON and her future husband HAROLD KNIGHT moved to Staithes and joined the Group. They married in 1903 and stayed in Staithes for ten years. In 1929 Laura Knight, as she now was, became THE FIRST WOMAN ARTIST TO BE MADE A DAME OF THE BRITISH EMPIRE, and in 1936, THE FIRST WOMAN TO BE ELECTED A FULL MEMBER OF THE ROYAL ACADEMY.

The railway that brought the artists to Staithes, the Whitby, Redcar and Middlesbrough Union Railway, crossed the Roxby Beck on a now vanished concrete and iron viaduct,

700 ft (213 m) long and 150 ft (46 m) high. The north parapet can still be seen; the south parapet has been levelled and made into the town's main public car park.

Whitby

Birthplace of English Christianity

WHITBY is a glorious old seaport where English poetry blossomed, where the English Church was fashioned, and from where Captain Cook sailed into immortality.

Cottages laced with narrow alleyways are piled high on the steep banks of the River Esk and tumble down the valley towards the harbour, where fishing boats bob and seagulls squabble.

Hilltop Church

At the summit of a steep stairway of 199 steps that climb up the east cliff, stands the sturdy parish church of ST

MARY, with a massive low tower and a slightly disconcerting mix of Norman, Gothic and Georgian architecture. Inside is a fantastical riot of box pews, galleries and pillars, all carved and constructed by shipbuilding craftsmen and crammed in haphazardly for different families at different times over the centuries – it's a rare example of a church interior completely untouched by Victorian restoration. The splendid Norman chancel arch is concealed by a gallery, a vast iron stove provides the heating, and big 18th-century windows flood the place with light. The whole thing is presided over by a whopping triple-decker pulpit built in 1748, and THE ONLY TRIPLE-DECKER PULPIT IN THE WORLD TO BE FOUND STANDING IN THE MIDDLE OF A CHURCH.

Christians from the south of England who followed the Roman traditions of St Augustine, and Celtic Christians from the north and west who believed in a more monastic form of Christianity, as introduced from Ireland. Their purpose was to decide which of these Christian disciplines should prevail.

King Oswy, ever practical, came down in favour of the Roman Church, whose leader Wilfrid claimed that his authority came direct from St Peter, holder of the keys to Heaven. 'Then I will obey St Peter,' the King declared, 'lest when I come to the Gates of Heaven there be none to open to me.'

This decision established the supremacy of the Roman Church in England, which would last for nearly 1,000 years until the English Reformation. Also fixed was the date of Easter – today we celebrate Easter when we do because of a judgement made 1,300 years ago by those wise Saxon bishops at the Synod of Whitby.

Synod of Whitby

Above the church lie the spectacular 13th-century ruins of WHITBY ABBEY, founded in 657 by St Hilda in thanks for King Oswy of Northumbria's victory over the heathen King Penda of Mercia. In 664 King Oswy convened THE FIRST-EVER CHURCH SYNOD in Whitby, bringing together

First English Poet

Another great figure at Whitby in those momentous times was the poet CAEDMON, an uneducated cowherd at the abbey who tended cattle on the cliff-top pastures and had a dream in which an angel commanded him to write a song about the Glory of Creation. His 'Song of Creation' was

THE FIRST ENGLISH POEM and Caedmon THE FIRST ENGLISH POET, the Father of the great English Literature that is so admired across the world. His vision of Creation influenced Milton's *Paradise Lost* and still resonates today in the lively debate between Creationists and those who tend towards the Theory of Evolution. A tall stone cross commemorating Caedmon, which was unveiled in 1898 by Poet Laureate Alfred Austin, stands in St Mary's churchyard. Carved on the base of the column are THE FIRST LINES OF POETRY EVER WRITTEN IN THE ENGLISH LANGUAGE:

> 'Now must we praise the
> Guardian of heaven's realm.
> The Creator's might and
> His mind's thought.'

Look Out

Between 1750 and 1840, Whitby was a major whaling port, a fact commemorated by a large whalebone arch that stands on the western cliffs near James Cook's statue. Whitby's most famous whaling captain was WILLIAM SCORESBY (1760–1829) who, in search of whales, sailed to 81 degrees 30 north, FURTHER NORTH THAN ANYONE HAD GONE PREVIOUSLY, a record he kept for 21 years. He also invented the 'CROW'S-NEST', a lookout fixed near the top of the mast

that protected seamen from severe weather conditions when on watch in the cold northern seas. His son WILLIAM SCORESBY JUNIOR (1789–1857) also became a whaling captain, achieving fame as a scientist in the field of magnetism and as an explorer of Greenland and the Arctic Seas. He ended up as the Bishop of Bradford.

Tourism

In the mid 19th century George Hudson, the Railway King, brought the railway to Whitby, tourism trailing in its wake. He began to develop Westcliff as the 'Bath of the North' but had only half finished the Royal Crescent when his money ran out – even so the Royal Crescent is still one of Whitby's sights today.

BRAM STOKER was staying in Westcliff, and researching in the Whitby Library, when he came up with the idea for COUNT DRACULA. In the story, Dracula comes ashore in Whitby in the form of a black dog and climbs the 199 steps to St Mary's churchyard, after his ship, a Russian cargo vessel called *Demeter*, is wrecked off the Whitby coast. This scene was no doubt inspired by a real incident that happened a few years earlier, when a ship called *Demetrius* was wrecked off Whitby, and its cargo of coffins laden with bodies was found floating in the sea. Whitby's Dracula connections were influential in the choice of Whitby as the location for a twice-yearly festival for Goths, held here since 1997.

Well, I never knew this about
THE NORTH RIDING COAST

SCARBOROUGH RAILWAY STATION boasts THE LONGEST SEAT IN ANY RAILWAY STATION IN THE WORLD, 456 ft (139 m) in length.

SCARBOROUGH BUILDING SOCIETY, formed in May 1846, is THE OLDEST BUILDING SOCIETY IN YORKSHIRE, and THE SECOND OLDEST IN BRITAIN. As a result of the credit crunch in 2008 it merged with the Skipton and is now trading as the Skipton Building Society.

Scarborough is THE LAST SEASIDE RESORT IN BRITAIN TO MAINTAIN A PROFESSIONAL ORCHESTRA.

STAITHES claims to have THE NARROWEST STREET IN YORKSHIRE, a passageway called DOG LOUP.

BOULBY CLIFF, 1 mile (1.6 km) west of Staithes, is THE HIGHEST SEA CLIFF IN ENGLAND, at 666 ft (203 m).

BOULBY MINE is THE SECOND DEEPEST MINE IN EUROPE, at 4,600 ft (1,400 m). It is THE ONLY POTASH MINE IN BRITAIN and produces over 1 million tons of potash and half a million tons of salt every year. There are over 600 miles (965 km) of tunnels, many of which run out under the North Sea. The mine was established by ICI in the 1960s and is now owned and run by Cleveland Potash, part of the ICL Fertilizer Group. There is also an underground laboratory inside the mine, which conducts experiments on the nature of Dark Matter, the invisible and unknown material said to make up a large percentage of the universe.

WHITBY has BRITAIN'S LARGEST DEPOSITS OF JET, a fossilised wood found in the nearby cliffs. WHITBY JET is regarded as THE FINEST JET IN THE WORLD, and for 60 years from the 1870s the jet industry flourished in the town. The fashion for jewellery made from jet was started by Queen Victoria, who wore it as a sign of bereavement after Prince Alfred died.

Every year, at 9 o'clock on a spring morning, a small crowd gathers in Whitby Harbour to watch the PLANTING OF THE PENNY HEDGE, a tradition that has been followed for 850 years. In 1159 three men were hunting boar in the woods of Esk valley when the animal took refuge in the small chapel of a hermit monk. The monk refused to let the men kill the boar, and they were so enraged that they set about the monk and savagely beat him. As he lay dying the monk forgave the men on the condition that every year, at sunrise on the morning of Ascension Eve, they planted a hedge in Whitby Harbour made from staves worth no more than a penny, and that would survive three tides. If it was washed away before three tides, then the men or their descendants would forfeit their land and property to the Abbot of Whitby. The penance is still faithfully carried out today and the hedge has yet to be swept away.

North York Moors

Rievaulx Abbey, the first Cistercian abbey in Yorkshire

Rievaulx

A Matchless Setting

'Bolton Abbey for the artist, Fountains Abbey for the historian, Rievaulx Abbey for the poet.' So the saying goes, and the poet William Cowper concurred, wishing that he could live in sight of Rievaulx for ever.

The first view of RIEVAULX ABBEY is one of those first views that remain in the heart for ever. No other abbey is blessed with a setting so divine. Gaunt, glowing, tall and utterly beau-tiful, it sits in glorious ruin in the romantic valley of its namesake, the River Rye. THE FIRST CISTERCIAN ABBEY IN YORKSHIRE, with YORK-SHIRE'S FIRST GOTHIC ARCHES, it was founded in 1131 by Walter L'Espec, who also built Helmsley Castle further down the valley. Within the grounds are the remnants of THE LARGEST ABBOT'S HOUSE IN ENGLAND.

The View from Above

Once explored, Rievaulx is perhaps best appreciated from the green RIEVAULX

TERRACES laid out on the hillside above, from where a gallery of matchless views of the ruins can be glimpsed down avenues cut through the trees. The ½ mile (0.8 km) walk along wide lawns overlooking the abbey runs between two Palladian 'temples', each with richly painted ceilings, one Doric, like a small version of the mausoleum at Castle Howard, the other Ionic and furnished in period style.

The terraces were laid out in 1758 by Thomas Duncombe to complement the terraces in the gardens of his ancestral home, Duncombe Park, overlooking Helmsley Castle.

Helmsley

A Good Start

HELMSLEY, still dominated by its ruined castle complete with bastions and built-in Elizabethan mansion, is a charming, timeless little town, centred on a cobbled square surrounded by coaching inns and half-timbered houses. Hearty types gather here to begin walking ENGLAND'S LONGEST FOOTPATH, THE 108-MILE (174 KM) CLEVELAND WAY, which ambles around the North York Moors to Filey.

Duncombe Park

The Duncombes came to Helmsley in 1689, when England's richest commoner, the goldsmith, banker and tax collector SIR CHARLES DUNCOMBE, paid £90,000 to the trustees of the murdered Duke of Buckingham for the purchase of the Helmsley estate. By 1713 a huge baroque house had been completed,

and Sir Charles's nephew Thomas moved in. The house has been through many adventures, including a major fire in 1879 and, even more devastating, 60 years as a girls' school, but it has now been restored to Lord Feversham of the Duncombe family, and can be visited along with the sumptuous parkland in which the house is set.

The grounds at DUNCOMBE PARK claim THE EARLIEST HA-HA, THE TALLEST ASH TREE IN ENGLAND (148 ft / 45 m high), and THE TALLEST LIME TREE IN ENGLAND (154 ft / 47 m high).

Mount Grace

Yorkshire's Charterhouse

MOUNT GRACE PRIORY IS THE BEST-PRESERVED CARTHUSIAN PRIORY, OR 'CHARTERHOUSE', IN ENGLAND, and THE ONLY CHARTERHOUSE IN YORK-SHIRE. It sits on the edge of the North York Moors, in a glorious setting, with woods climbing the hills behind and with far-reaching views across the Vale of York to the Pennines in front.

The priory was founded in 1398 by Thomas Holland, 1st and only Duke of Surrey, a nephew of Richard II. He was executed in 1400 for conspiring against Henry IV, and 12 years later his body was brought to the priory he had founded and buried there.

Unlike most monastic orders, who lived together in communities, Carthusian monks lived alone, virtually as hermits, each with his own two-storey cell and a small patch of garden. Every cell had its own door

Kilburn

on to the courtyard, and food was passed through a hatch in the wall, set at a right angle so that the recipient couldn't see the monk who was serving him. One of these cells has been reconstructed, along with the very advanced sanitation system, to give an idea of what it must have been like to live at Mount Grace in the 14th and 15th centuries.

The Bells, the Bells

The priory guesthouse was turned into a comfortable manor house in 1654 by Thomas Lascelles and in the 19th century was refashioned in Arts and Crafts style by SIR LOWTHIAN BELL (1816–1904), founder of the Clarence Iron Works on Teesside, who was also responsible for preserving the priory ruins and reconstructing the monk's cell. Sir Lowthian's granddaughter was GERTRUDE BELL, the writer and traveller known as the 'Queen of Iraq', who helped to draw the map of the Middle East. She grew up here and so loved Mount Grace that she buried her beloved dog, Tundra, in the grounds.

One of the treasures of Mount Grace Priory was THE ONLY SURVIVING MANUSCRIPT OF THE FIRST AUTOBIOGRAPHY IN THE ENGLISH LANGUAGE, THE BOOK OF MARGERY KEMPE, written between 1438 and 1442. It is now in the British Library.

A Horse . . .

The KILBURN WHITE HORSE, carved into the turf near Roulston Scar, south of Sutton Bank, is THE LARGEST AND MOST NORTHERLY WHITE HORSE IN BRITAIN. Created in 1857 by local schoolmaster JOHN HODGSON, with help from his pupils, it measures 318 ft (97 m) long and 220 ft (67 m) high. It was funded by Thomas Taylor, a merchant and native of Kilburn, who was inspired by a visit to the Uffington White Horse in Berkshire. The Kilburn White Horse can be seen over 45 miles (72 km) away in Lincolnshire, and during the Second World War it was covered up so as not to provide a landmark for enemy bombers.

. . . and a Mouse

Below the white horse sits the village of KILBURN, birthplace of the Yorkshire furniture maker ROBERT 'MOUSEMAN' THOMPSON (1876–1955).

Thompson taught himself to make furniture out of English oak, in classic 17th-century English styles, using traditional tools. In the uncertain early days while he was struggling to build up the business, one of his colleagues observed that 'we shall probably all end up as poor as church mice', whereupon Thompson carved a mouse on the piece of church furniture they were working on. It became his trademark and can be found somewhere on all his work – searching for the mouse in the many churches he furnished, amongst them Selby Abbey, Bridlington Priory and Holy Trinity in Hull, can make a diverting pastime for adults or children.

Robert Thompson's workshop in Kilburn still produces fine oak furniture today, and there is a visitor centre and museum that tells of his life and works.

Pickering

Hidden Treasure

PICKERING's parish church stands hidden at the top of the main street,

and is reached by a variety of steep stone stairways that toil up through trees and past old houses. It is a majestic building that has developed out of a Norman church, but there is little outside to prepare you for the breathtaking surprise that awaits inside when you switch on the lighting. High up on the walls, disappearing into the gloom, is 'THE MOST COMPLETE COLLECTION OF MEDIEVAL WALL PAINTINGS IN ENGLAND', showing scenes from the Bible, the martyrdom of St Thomas à Becket, and St George and the Dragon. At one time they were whitewashed over in case they encouraged idolatry, but happily they were rediscovered in 1876. They are certainly vivid and extraordinary.

In the sanctuary hangs a memorial tablet to Pickering-born surveyors and cartographers ROBERT AND NICHOLAS KING, father and son, who emigrated to America in 1790 and helped plan the layout of America's capital city, Washington DC. Nicholas was appointed as THE FIRST SURVEYOR OF WASHINGTON DC, founded WASHINGTON'S FIRST PUBLIC LIBRARY, and became a trustee of the city's school board, alongside Thomas Jefferson. Robert made maps for the War Board, one of which was used by the Lewis and Clark expedition of 1804–6.

'A Quaint Old Railway'

Pickering is the southern terminus for the NORTH YORKSHIRE MOORS RAILWAY, which runs for 18 miles (29 km) from Pickering to Grosmont and is THE SECOND-LONGEST HERITAGE STEAM RAILWAY LINE IN BRITAIN (after the 20-mile (32 km) long West Somerset Steam Railway). It comprises the middle section of the former line connecting Malton, Pickering and Whitby, which fell victim to the Beeching cuts in 1965. Charles Dickens rode on the original line and declared it 'a quaint old railway'.

Goathland – Hogwarts

Perhaps the best-known station on the North Yorkshire Moors Railway is GOATHLAND, almost unchanged since it was built in 1865, which portrays HOGSMEADE STATION, the stop for Hogwarts School in the Harry Potter films.

Goathland – Heartbeat

Goathland is also the setting for the village of AIDENSFIELD in the Sunday night ITV soap opera HEARTBEAT. Many of the landmarks from the series are recognisable, including the village shop (Aidensfield stores), the Goathland Hotel (Aidensfield Arms) and the village garage, which is decked out in the guise of Scripps garage and funeral parlour, and often has the distinctive blue and white Ford Anglia police car from the series sitting on the forecourt.

The name Aidensfield was inspired by an image of St Aidan on a stained-glass window in Goathland parish church.

Heartbeat itself was inspired by the Constable series of books written by author NICOLAS RHEA, who was himself (under his real name Peter Walker) a bobby in various locations around the North Riding.

Kirkdale

A Saxon Sundial

'Orm the son of Gamal bought St
Gregory's Church when it was all
utterly broke and fallen, and caused
it to be made anew from the
ground, to Christ and St Gregory, in
the days of King Edward and in the
days of Earl Tosti. Hawarth wrought
me, and Brand the Prior.'

This inscription, THE LONGEST
ENGRAVED INSCRIPTION IN SAXON
ENGLISH IN BRITAIN, can be found
surrounding a sundial above the door
of ST GREGORY'S MINSTER at KIRK-
DALE. The whole ensemble can be
dated to around 1055 when Earl Tostig,
brother of Harold Godwin, later King
Harold, was Earl of Northumbria.
Tostig would later be banished from
England for the murder of the Gamal
mentioned in the inscription. He
returned in 1066 along with the King
of Norway, Harald Hardrada, to challenge King Harold at the Battle of
Stamford Bridge.

St Gregory's Minster, thought to be
the burial place of King Ethelwald, son
of King Oswy of Northumbria, sounds
as though it must be a mighty place,
but is in fact a small, rather topsy-turvy
building, set in dark woods, on land
sloping down to the Hodge Beck.

An English Hippopotamus

Below the church, on the other side
of the beck, which here runs through
a deep quarry, is a hidden cave discovered in 1821. Contained within are the
bones of animals no longer found in
Britain, such as tigers, elephants and
wolves. KIRKDALE CAVE is today
recognised as THE MOST NORTHERLY
LOCATION WHERE HIPPOPOTAMUS
REMAINS HAVE EVER BEEN FOUND.

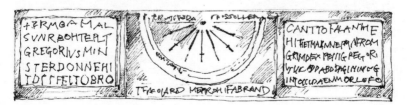

Egton Bridge

Last Martyr

EGTON BRIDGE was the birthplace of FATHER NICOLAS POSTGATE (1599–1679), THE LAST ENGLISH CATHOLIC MARTYR, who was born in KIRKDALE HOUSE near the bridge. Ordained as a priest in 1628, he spent his life wandering the moors disguised as a pedlar in order to minister to his scattered flock of Catholic faithful, at a time when the Catholic faith was suppressed. For the last 20 years of his life he lived at the Hermitage in Ugthorpe, near Whitby. In 1678, during the furore raised by Titus Oates and his 'Popish Plot', Father Nicolas was betrayed by a local excise man, John Reeves, and arrested while baptising a baby at Red Barn Farm. After a show trial he was hung, drawn and quartered at York on 7 August 1679, when he was 80 years old. The crucifix he wore at his execution is now in Ampleforth Abbey. The treacherous Reeves was later found drowned in a pond near Sleights, where no fish has been caught since.

Playing Gooseberry

Egton Bridge is now known as the setting for THE OLDEST GOOSEBERRY SHOW IN BRITAIN, established in 1800 by the Old Gooseberry Society, and held every year in August. In 2009

Bryan Nellist won first prize with THE BIGGEST GOOSEBERRY EVER SEEN IN BRITAIN, weighing in at 2.19 oz, or 62 grams.

Lastingham

Unique Crypt

The church at LASTINGHAM sits above the centre of the village, which lies in a wooded fold of the moors. A monastery was founded here by St Cedd and St Chad, brothers from Lindisfarne, in about AD 654. St Cedd was buried here when he died in 664, not long after attending the Synod of Whitby. In 1078 the Normans built a crypt over St Cedd's grave, and in the following couple of centuries a church was raised around it. The crypt has remained untouched and is unique in an English country church, being THE MOST COMPLETE AND COMPLEX CHAPEL OF ITS KIND TO HAVE SURVIVED ANYWHERE. It has an apse,

a chancel, a nave and two aisles, and the arches are supported by squat pillars with carved capitals. The altar is a block of carved stone thought to have been a Roman incense altar, and much of the stonework comes from the original Saxon monastery. It is perhaps the most peaceful place in Yorkshire, rivalled only by St Wilfrid's crypt at Ripon.

Well, I never knew this about

THE NORTH YORK MOORS

The NORTH YORK MOORS are THE LARGEST AREA OF HEATHER MOORLAND IN ENGLAND.

Hidden away in woods north of Whitby are two MULGRAVE CASTLES, one a Norman structure now in ruins and the other an 18th-century house set in grounds laid out by Capability Brown, ancient seat of the Marquess of Normanby. Between 1859 and 1865 the house was occupied by the MAHARA-JAH DHULEEP SINGH, who gave the Koh-i-Nor diamond to Queen Victoria, and who was exiled to England by the British Raj. Amongst the Maharajah's entourage were a number of elephants that were occasionally to be seen exercising on the North York Moors.

When he was raised to the House of Lords, former Prime Minister HAROLD WILSON took the title BARON WILSON OF RIEVAULX.

THE WORLD'S FIRST STAINLESS-STEEL MAYPOLE can be found on the village green at SINNINGTON.

EBBERSTON HALL, a Palladian villa sitting on the edge of woods to the north of the road between Pickering and Scarborough, was built in 1718, and is known as 'THE SMALLEST STATELY HOME IN ENGLAND'.

MALLYAN SPOUT, near Goathland, is THE TALLEST WATERFALL ON THE NORTH YORKSHIRE MOORS, 60 ft (18 m) high.

The little moorland village of GLAIS-DALE, once an important centre for ironstone mining, is today visited for its packhorse bridge, which was built in 1619 by THOMAS FERRIS and is known as BEGGAR'S BRIDGE. As a young man, Ferris had to swim across the River Esk to tryst with his love, the daughter of a wealthy squire, and suffered much abuse from her father for his bedraggled appearance. So he sailed away to make his fortune on the Spanish Main, and on his return not only married the squire's daughter but built the bridge we see there today so that no other young lovers should have to bear such indignities.

NORTH RIDING DALES

Bolton Castle – fortress fit for a queen

Wensleydale

Wensleydale is the name given to the valley of the River Ure, and is one of the few dales to be named after a village (Wensley) rather than a river.

Hawes

At the head of Wensleydale lies the small market town of HAWES, where WENSLEYDALE CHEESE is produced. Cheese-making was first brought to Wensleydale by French monks who settled at Fors, near Hawes, in 1150, before moving to Jervaulx Abbey further downstream. The recipe was learned by local farmers who kept the tradition alive, although they preferred to use cow's milk rather than sheep's milk as originally used by the monks. Today Wensleydale cheese is made in Hawes by Wensleydale Dairy Products. Sales rocketed in the 1990s when it was revealed on film that Wensleydale was the favourite cheese of the cartoon characters Wallace and Gromit.

A mile outside Hawes is the stunningly beautiful HAWDRAW FORCE, THE HIGHEST UNBROKEN WATERFALL ABOVE GROUND IN ENGLAND, with a straight fall of 100 ft (30 m). It used to be possible to stand behind the falls and watch a million rainbows formed by the sun shining through the curtain of water but, alas, this wonderful experience, which enchanted Turner, Wordsworth and Ruskin, is now prohibited. KEVIN COSTNER bathed in the pool beneath the falls in his role as Robin Hood in the 1991 film *Robin Hood: Prince of Thieves.*

GAYLE, south of Hawes, is a tiny village with an old bridge, a turbulent mountain stream – and THE OLDEST UNALTERED COTTON MILL IN BRITAIN. It was built in 1785 and brought the Industrial Revolution to the Dales. In 1878 the waterwheel was replaced by a double-vortex turbine, which is still there and is believed to be THE OLDEST OPERATIONAL WATER TURBINE IN ITS ORIGINAL SITUATION IN THE WORLD.

Askrigg

ASKRIGG, a village of tall houses and narrow cobbled streets, found fame in the late 1970s for portraying the fictional village of Darrowby, home

of vet James Herriot, in the BBC television series *All Creatures Great and Small.* Skeldale House, which played Herriot's surgery, stands across the road from St Oswald's Church, and the King's Arms appeared in many episodes as the Drover's Arms. The real surgery is in Thirsk (*see* Thirsk).

Not far from Askrigg, with glorious views over Wensleydale, lies NAPPA HALL, ancestral home of the Metcalfe family, prominent in Wensleydale for over 500 years. James Metcalfe was presented with the Nappa estate by Sir Richard Scrope of Castle Bolton, after they had fought together at the Battle of Agincourt in 1415. The hall was built around 1450 by Sir Thomas Metcalfe and remained in the family until 2008. Virtually unchanged, it is ONE OF THE FEW SURVIVING FORTIFIED HOUSES IN YORKSHIRE.

Aysgarth

In the 1930s ALF WIGHT (James Herriot) and his new wife came for their honeymoon to the tiny village of CARPERBY, THE FIRST VILLAGE IN THE YORKSHIRE DALES TO WIN THE BEST KEPT VILLAGE TITLE (1959).

From Carperby it is but a short walk to the delightful triple falls at AYSGARTH, where the River Ure, hemmed in by woods, tumbles noisily over a staircase of broad limestone ledges. A fine stone bridge with a single arch of 70 ft (21 m) spans the river between the upper and middle falls beside an old cotton mill that provided the yarn for the red shirts of Garibaldi's Italian Legion. Looking down on this scene is Aysgarth Church, which sits in what is said to be ENGLAND'S LARGEST CHURCHYARD, of something over 4 acres (1.62 ha).

The upper falls were the setting for the fight scene between Robin Hood and Little John in *Robin Hood: Prince of Thieves.*

Bolton Castle

High on the hillside, four square and massive, BOLTON CASTLE looms over Wensleydale, awe-inspiring even in ruin. A petite 14th-century church cowers beneath the walls, while the handsome little village of Castle Bolton pays court nearby. The castle was built between 1378 and 1399 by Sir Richard Scrope, Lord Chancellor for Richard II, and as well as being a powerful fortress it was one of the most luxurious homes of its day, with separate apartments, plumbing that

continued in use until Victorian times and chimneys – 'the smoke was conveyed from the hearth in the hall, through tunnils through the walls and no other louvers'. Fit for a Queen, you might think, and indeed Mary Queen of Scots was held prisoner here for six months when she first fled to England. The very bed in which she slept can still be seen in her bedroom, which overlooks Wensleydale.

Bolton Castle is now owned by Lord Bolton, a direct descendant of the Scropes, and is open to the public.

Wensley

Inside HOLY TRINITY CHURCH at WENSLEY, 'Queen of Wensleydale', is the opulent SCROPE PEW, installed by the 3rd Duke of Bolton for his wife Lavinia. She was an opera singer, and the pew is the very opera box in which the Duke was sitting when he fell in love while watching her perform. The back of the pew is part of a richly carved 16th-century screen, brought here from the Scrope chantry in Easby Abbey, near Richmond, after the Dissolution of the Monasteries. It is adorned with the coat of arms of George III and, on the reverse, the arms of the Scropes, reckoned to be THE OLDEST COAT OF ARMS IN ENGLAND after those of the Royal Family. By the door is a panelled wooden alms box, a reliquary brought from Easby, and ONE OF ONLY TWO SUCH RELIQUARIES IN ENGLAND, the other being at Bodmin in Cornwall.

Middleham

Windsor of the North

MIDDLEHAM'S Norman castle, with ONE OF THE BIGGEST KEEPS IN ENGLAND, still dominates the pleasant market town at its feet. When the castle came into the hands of the mighty Neville family they refashioned it into the most splendid and luxurious pile in Yorkshire, another Windsor of the North, and made it their chief stronghold.

In 1472 Richard, Duke of York, the future Richard III, married Anne Neville, daughter of Richard Neville, better known as Warwick the 'King-maker', and they made Middleham their home. The following year their son Edward was born in the round tower at the south-west corner of the curtain wall, now known as the Prince's Tower. And here Edward died in 1484, aged 11, having just been invested as Prince of Wales, after his father's accession to the throne. The Prince's body was taken to SHERIFF HUTTON, where his mother was staying, and he was buried in the church there, THE ONLY PRINCE OF WALES TO BE BURIED IN A PARISH CHURCH.

An interesting feature inside Middleham Castle is the circular horse pit used for grinding corn. The horse is still very important to Middleham – although the hoofbeats heard in the town today belong not to workhorses but rather to race-horses, as they make their way to the gallops on High Moor.

In what is known as the Swine Market, underneath the north wall of the castle, there is a block of stone carved with a boar's head, possibly representing the white boar of Richard III.

Swaledale

The RIVER SWALE, which is THE FASTEST-FLOWING RIVER IN ENGLAND, rises just to the east of Nine Standards Rigg, the prominent ridge on the border with Westmorland where nine tall cairns stand watch over the Dales and the Eden Valley.

It then carves a narrow valley down to the village of Keld, flows by numerous lonely stone barns to Muker, Gunnerside and Reeth, and sweeps below majestic Richmond Castle, perched on its high bluff, before meandering across farmland to join the River Ure, fresh out of Wensleydale. Together they form the Ouse, which then merges with the Trent to become the mighty Humber.

Richmond

'On Richmond Hill there lives a Lass,
More bright than May Day morn,
Whose charms all other maids surpass,
A Rose without a Thorn.'

So wrote Leonard McNally about Frances l'Anson, who lived at Hill House in Richmond, and in 1787 became his wife.

RICHMOND was a romantic town then and is a romantic town now, with its steep, cobbled market square, crooked alleyways and handsome Georgian shops and houses. At the heart of the square the medieval Holy Trinity Church serves as the Regimental Museum of the Green Howards, who were so named after the colour of the facings on their uniform and the name of their Colonel during the War of Austrian Succession in 1744, Charles Howard.

Oldest Castle Walls

RICHMOND CASTLE was built in 1080 to guard the river crossing at the entrance to Swaledale, and has THE OLDEST ORIGINAL CASTLE WALLS STILL STANDING IN BRITAIN. Also, the castle's great hall, known as SCOLLAND'S HALL, is THE OLDEST STONE HALL IN BRITAIN. William I of Scotland (William the Lion) was held prisoner here after the Battle of Alnwick in 1174. The view of the river and the town from the top of the keep, 114 ft (35 m) in height and perched above the precipice, is dizzying.

Oldest Theatre

Narrow Friar's Wynd leads off the square to Richmond's hidden gem, the Georgian THEATRE ROYAL. Opened in 1788, it later fell on hard times and for a while was used as a warehouse before becoming a working theatre again in 1968. The interior is gorgeous, with the original galleries and boxes lovingly restored, and it is THE OLDEST WORKING THEATRE IN ITS ORIGINAL FORM AND PREMISES IN EUROPE.

Easby

Colours and Drums

Reached by a lovely riverside walk from Richmond are the ruins of EASBY ABBEY, founded in 1152 by Roald, the Constable of Richmond Castle, for the Premonstratensian Order, or White Canons. The first of the Scropes of Bolton Castle is reputedly buried here.

According to legend, there is a secret tunnel running between the abbey and the castle, which many have looked for but no one has found. At the time of the Napoleonic Wars some soldiers lowered a drummer boy down the castle well to see if they could locate it by following the sound of his beating drum. He apparently could be heard until they reached the river, at which point the drumming stopped and the boy was never seen again. Visitors to the abbey, however, can sometimes make out a weak, melancholy drumbeat emanating from somewhere under the ruins . . .

Set back amongst the trees that garland the abbey grounds is the little CHURCH OF ST AGATHA, here since early Norman days and filled with magnificent wall paintings from the 13th century, comparable to those at Pickering. There is also a replica of the Easby Cross, a rare 7th-century stone cross carved with birds and animals and a representation of Jesus with the Disciples, which was found embedded in the church walls. The original was rescued, pieced back together and sent to the Victoria and Albert Museum, where it now resides.

Church of St Agatha

Aske

The Great Match

A short drive out of Richmond takes you past the vast gate of ASKE HALL, ancestral home of the (de) Aske family (*see* Pilgrimage of Grace, page 55), and now the family seat of the Marquess of Zetland, whose ancestor Sir Lawrence Dundas bought the Hall in 1763. The gate is known as the VOLTIGEUR GATE and commemorates the famous racehorse owned by the 2nd Earl of Zetland, which won the Derby and the St Leger in 1850.

The two most successful racehorses of the day were VOLTIGEUR and his great rival THE FLYING DUTCHMAN, owned by the Earl of Eglinton and bred by Henry Vansittart of Kirkleatham. When Voltigeur beat The Flying Dutchman in a straight fight in the Doncaster Gold Cup of 1850 the Earl of Eglinton was apparently so shocked that he had to be restored with brandy. Thus fortified, he immediately issued a challenge to the Earl of Zetland. 'We must have a return!' he cried. 'Indeed,' replied Lord Zetland. 'A straight match on the best course in the country – York. Shall we say over two miles for a thousand pounds?' 'You're on!'

And so came about the Great Match of 1851. Thousands lined the rails at York as the two noble horses flew round the course. They were neck and neck as they passed the grandstand, but The Flying Dutchman crossed the finishing line just ahead of Voltigeur – the Earl of Eglinton was avenged! The Earl of Zetland was magnanimous in defeat. 'But,' he said, 'you will always remember the only horse ever to beat your Dutchman!'

The rivalry had a happy ending. Voltigeur's son Vedette was mated with The Flying Dutchman's daughter, The Flying Duchess, and the union produced GALOPIN, who won the Derby in 1875.

In 1950 the GREAT VOLTIGEUR STAKES was inaugurated at York to celebrate the centenary of Voltigeur's St Leger triumph, and is now run every year in August.

Stable block at Aske Hall

Bowes

Academical

'The first gravestone I stumbled on that dreary afternoon was over a boy who had died suddenly. I suppose his heart broke. He died in this wretched place, and I think his ghost put Smike into my mind on the spot.'

So wrote Charles Dickens when he visited the eerie churchyard of St Giles in BOWES, overlooked by its gaunt ruined castle, on a cold grey morning in February 1838. The grave was that of George Ashton Taylor, immortalised for ever by Dickens as Smike in *Nicholas Nickleby*, but who died in 1822 at just 19, a victim of the harsh conditions at the local school, Shaw's Academy, where there was only cold water to bathe in and no towels and no holidays.

Dickens had come to Bowes to investigate for himself the truth about the notorious 'Yorkshire' schools, where unwanted children were sent to

be 'educated' by cruel and unscrupulous bullies. He stayed at the Ancient Unicorn Inn and called in at Shaw's Academy hoping to be shown around, but a suspicious William Shaw, the headmaster, met Dickens with a dead eye and refused him entry. That brief meeting gave Dickens not only his grim Dotheboys Hall but also his tyrant headmaster Wackford Squeers.

Although Bowes today is a rather more cheerful place, it is still windswept and grey, and isolated enough that you can imagine the scene, and shudder at how those poor boys must have felt as they got off the coach at the Ancient Unicorn and gazed at the forbidding walls of their new home. The Ancient Unicorn is now the village pub. Smike's grave is still there, ironically not far from that of his tormentor William Shaw. Dotheboys Hall, in reality a rather elegant, rambling two-storey house, has been converted into private accommodation and like Dickens, you can't get in.

Well, I never knew this
about
THE NORTH RIDING DALES

MICKLE FELL 2,585ft (788 m) is THE HIGHEST POINT IN YORKSHIRE.

COVERHAM, near Middleham, was the birthplace of MILES COVERDALE (1488–1569), who produced and published THE FIRST COMPLETE ENGLISH TRANSLATION OF THE BIBLE, in 1535. Henry VIII ordered that a Coverdale Bible should be displayed in every church, chained to a pew, so that every Englishman should have access to the Bible.

THE TAN HILL INN, reached by a winding road from Keld in Swaledale, stands at 1,732 ft (528 m) above sea level and is THE HIGHEST PUB IN ENGLAND. It was built in 1737 to serve the men mining for coal in the surrounding hills. In January 2010 some 60 New Year's Eve revellers were trapped at the inn by heavy snowstorms. They survived by playing cards and drinking beer in what was dubbed BRITAIN'S LONGEST-RUNNING NEW YEAR'S EVE PARTY.

On the hills above Richmond the track of Richmond racecourse can still be seen, along with the sad remains of the grandstand built by John Carr of York in 1777. The course closed in 1891.

The RIVER BAIN, which carries water 2½ miles (4 km) from YORKSHIRE'S LARGEST NATURAL LAKE, LAKE SEMERWATER, through the village of Bainbridge to the River Ure, is believed to be THE SHORTEST RIVER IN ENGLAND.

NORTH RIDING HILLS AND VALES

Castle Howard – Brideshead Revisited

Thirsk

All Creatures Great and Small

The unspoiled market town of THIRSK was home to the author and vet ALF WIGHT (1916–95), known to the world as JAMES HERRIOT. He joined the practice of Donald Sinclair (alias Siegfried Farnon, played by Robert Hardy in the TV series) in 1940, and continued both to work as a vet and to write of his experiences until his death in 1995.

The surgery, in a fine Georgian house with a red door at No. 23 Kirkgate in Thirsk, has been fitted out as it would have looked in the 1950s, as has the rest of the house, and it is now run as a fascinating museum known as 'THE WORLD OF JAMES HERRIOT'.

Opposite the 'The World of James Herriot', at No. 14 Kirkgate, is the house where THOMAS LORD (1755–1832), the founder of Lord's cricket ground in London, was born. It is now the town museum.

Coxwold

Tristram Shandy

COXWOLD is set in a narrow valley between the hills, its gently sloping main street lined with stone houses. The church, with its striking octagonal tower, watches over the village from a high green mound and against the south wall is the headstone of Coxwold's most famous curate, LAURENCE STERNE (1713–68), author of *The Life and Opinions of Tristram Shandy, Gentleman.*

Sterne came to Coxwold in 1760, towards the end of his life, and lived a little way up from the church, across the road, in the low, rambling, pink brick parsonage, where he finished *Tristram Shandy* and wrote *A Sentimental Journey.* He playfully named the house SHANDY HALL in honour of his comic masterpiece, and it is today run as a museum in his memory.

Inside the church where Sterne preached are a gallery, low box pews with doors, and a veritable maelstrom of monuments, most of them to the Bellasis family, who took the title of Fauconberg in 1627.

Newburgh Priory

Oliver Cromwell, I Presume?

The home of the Fauconbergs, NEWBURGH ABBEY, lies 1 mile (1.6 km) outside Coxwold. It is a comfortable Tudor house converted from an Augustinian Priory, which was sold by Henry VIII to his chaplain Anthony de Bellasis at the Dissolution of the Monasteries.

Thomas Bellasis, 1st Earl Fauconberg, whose splendid tomb graces the church at Coxwold, married Oliver Cromwell's daughter Mary, and there is a small, bare attic room in a dark corner of Newburgh Abbey where the bones of the Protector are said to be stored, in a rough brick depository covered by wooden planks. Oliver Cromwell's body was dug up from Westminster Abbey by Charles II, and his head removed and stuck on a pike outside Parliament. The head ended up in Sidney Sussex College, Cambridge, but no one knows what happened to the rest of Cromwell's body. It is rumoured that his bones were collected by his daughter Mary and brought to Newburgh, but the little brick tomb there has never been opened and keeps its secret well. Edward VII visited Newburgh when he was Prince of Wales, and in one of the planks over the tomb there is a hole made by the Prince in an unsuccessful attempt to see what lay inside.

Castle Howard

Brideshead Revisited

CASTLE HOWARD is one Yorkshire's biggest houses, and the central dome was THE FIRST DOME OF ITS KIND TO BE BUILT FOR A PRIVATE HOUSE IN BRITAIN. The house was begun in 1700 for Charles, the 3rd Earl of Carlisle (1669–1738), who hired John Vanbrugh as the architect. Vanbrugh was a soldier turned successful playwright and had never designed a house before, but he was persuaded by the Earl to take on the commission over a game of cards at the Kit Kat Club, of which they were both members. It was 100 years before the whole building was complete. In 1940 much of it was gutted by fire, but it was restored by George Howard, who

Newburgh Priory

inherited the estate after his two brothers were killed in the Second World War.

The gardens cover 1,000 acres (405 ha) and include a circular mausoleum by Nicholas Hawksmoor, regarded as THE FINEST MAUSOLEUM IN ENGLAND. Horace Walpole claimed that it was so magnificent that he was tempted to be buried in there alive.

Castle Howard has played the role of Brideshead, the great house in Evelyn Waugh's novel *Brideshead Revisited*, on two occasions, once for the 1981 television adaptation by John Mortimer, starring Jeremy Irons, Anthony Andrews and Laurence Olivier, and again in 2008 for the Hollywood film version.

Old Byland

Abbey Facts

In 1322 the forces of the Scots King Robert the Bruce fought a fierce battle against the English on SCAWTON MOOR, between the little village of OLD BYLAND and Rievaulx Abbey, where Edward II was staying. The English were routed and Edward had to flee ignominiously, leaving all his belongings behind at Rievaulx.

Hidden behind old cottages in Old Byland on the North Yorkshire Moors is a tiny Norman church, which incorporates the remains of a Saxon chapel

and sports a Norman font given by Cistercian monks who had settled at nearby Tylas. The monks were forced to move from Tylas because their bell-ringing disturbed the monks at Rievaulx, and they eventually settled at Byland Abbey near Coxwold and built BYLAND ABBEY, which has THE LARGEST CLOISTERS IN ENGLAND. Surviving treasures include 13th-century floor tiles from the church, and ENGLAND'S ONLY STONE LECTERN BASE, from the chapter house. The altar from Byland is now in Ampleforth Abbey.

Ampleforth

AMPLEFORTH COLLEGE, founded in 1803 by Benedictine monks, is THE LARGEST PRIVATE CATHOLIC CO-EDUCA-TIONAL BOARDING SCHOOL IN BRITAIN.

ST MARTIN'S, AMPLEFORTH, the prep school for Ampleforth College, is housed in the Elizabethan GILLING CASTLE, overlooking the nearby village of Gilling, an old home of the Fairfax family. The stained-glass

Some distinguished Old Amplefordians

Cardinal Hume
18th Duke of Norfolk
King Letsie III of Lesotho
Sir Anthony Bamford, managing director of JCB
Actor Rupert Everett
Actor and Oscar-winning writer Julian Fellowes
Sculptor of *The Angel of the North* Antony Gormley
Brigadier Andrew Parker Bowles
Travel writer William Dalrymple
Rugby player Lawrence Dallaglio
Lord Lovat (1911–95), founder of the Commandos
David Stirling (1915–90), founder of the SAS

heraldic shields of the Fairfaxes from the Great Hall were sold to William Randolph Hearst in 1930, but retrieved on his death in 1951, still in their packing cases, and put back in place. The exquisite Elizabethan Long Gallery is now in the Bowes Museum at Barnard Castle.

Well, I never knew this about

THE NORTH RIDING HILLS AND VALES

The capital of the North Riding is NORTHALLERTON.

NUNNINGTON HALL, near Helmsley, is a lovely Tudor manor house, remodelled in 1655. It was at one time the home of DR ROBERT HUICKE, physician to Henry VIII, and the man who had to break the news to Elizabeth I that she could never have children. The house is now run by the National Trust.

BENINGBROUGH HALL, another National Trust property, 8 miles (13 km) north-west of York, is an early Georgian red-brick house, built by William Thornton for John Bourchier, on the site of the Bourchier's original Elizabethan manor house, as a wedding present for John's wife, Mary Bellwood. The Bourchier heraldic badge is the shape of a 'granny knot', and hence in heraldic terms a granny knot is known as a 'Bourchier knot' – a fine example of which can be found on the tomb of Archbishop Bourchier in Canterbury Cathedral. Archbishop Bourchier crowned three kings, Edward IV, Richard III and Henry VII.

Beningbrough Hall

The entrance to HOVINGHAM HALL, ancestral home of the Duchess of

Hovingham Hall

Kent's family the Worsleys, is through a riding school. THOMAS WORSLEY, who designed and built the house, was mad on horses and spent so much time and money on the stables that he only had enough left for a small residential wing. The lawn outside the house is THE OLDEST PRIVATE CRICKET FIELD IN ENGLAND.

YORKSHIRE LAVENDER at TERRINGTON, west of Malton, is BRITAIN'S MOST NORTHERLY LAVENDER FARM.

ROKEBY PARK, built in 1730, was made famous by Sir Walter Scott in his poem *Rokeby*. The house was owned by Scott's friend JOHN MORRIT, who jokingly complained that the poem attracted far too many visitors to his home. Rokeby Park was the home of the last surviving nude painting by the 17th-century Spanish artist DIEGO VELAZQUEZ, which became known as the 'Rokeby Venus'. It was sold to the National Gallery in London in 1906 and was badly damaged in an attack by the suffragette Mary Richardson in 1914, in protest at the arrest of Emmeline Pankhurst. It was successfully restored.

The driveway to CASTLE HOWARD passes through THE LONGEST AVENUE OF LIME TREES IN EUROPE.

West Riding

CAPITAL: WAKEFIELD

AIREDALE

Leeds Town Hall, home to the largest 3-manual organ in Europe

Bingley

All Locked Up

THE FIVE RISE LOCKS on the Leeds & Liverpool canal at BINGLEY from THE STEEPEST FLIGHT OF LOCKS IN BRITAIN, with a rise of 59 ft 2 ins (18.03 m) over a distance of 320 ft (98 m) – that is a gradient of roughly 1 in 5.

The first boat to use the locks when they opened in 1774 negotiated the descent in 28 minutes. The gates at the bottom of the rise are THE TALLEST LOCK GATES IN BRITAIN. The system is so complex that it requires a full-time lock-keeper, and the locks are padlocked at night. A little way downstream are the slightly less daunting Three Rise Locks.

Britain's largest breed of terrier, the AIREDALE TERRIER, was bred first in Bingley in the 1850s.

Cottingley

Away with the Fairies

The name of COTTINGLEY, a small village lying to the south of Bingley, was made famous in the 1920s by the strange tale of the Cottingley Fairies. In 1918, 16-year-old ELSIE WRIGHT and her cousin, 10-year-old FRANCES GRIFFITHS, on being scolded for arriving home soaking wet, claimed to have fallen into the beck at the bottom of the garden while playing with fairies. In order to prove it they went back to the beck and took a picture showing Frances watching what looked like a group of fairies dancing on the branches of a tree in front of her. They took another picture a few weeks later showing Elsie playing with a gnome-like figure, and insisted that the photos were not a trick.

When Frances's mother Polly showed the pictures to her branch of the Theosophical Society there was uproar, and the photographs were sent away to experts who pronounced them genuine. The girls produced three more images, and even Sir Arthur Conan Doyle, the creator of Sherlock Holmes, was convinced the photos were real. The story went around the world when he published them in the *Strand Magazine*, and later wrote a book called *The Coming of the Fairies* which aroused much ridicule. Sir Arthur went to his grave believing in fairies, and it wasn't until 1981 that Elise and Frances admitted the pictures were a hoax – although Frances maintained until she died in 1986 that there really were fairies in the garden at Cottingley . . .

The 1997 film *Fairy Tale: A True Story*, starring Peter O'Toole, is based on the story of the Cottingley Fairies.

Bradford

Wool Capital of the World

BRADFORD, 'Wool Capital of the World,' until as recently as the Second World War, sits in a bowl, surrounded by hills, with streets running down from the ring road to the centre like the spokes of a wheel.

Although pockmarked by empty

building plots, the city centre still boasts an impressive array of gargantuan Victoriana such as the colossal City Hall, covered in the statues of 35 monarchs, including Oliver Cromwell, and with a tower 220 ft (67 m) high inspired by the Palazzo Vecchio in Florence. Then there is the Wool Exchange, where wool merchants from all over the world used to gather, now a bookshop, and St George's Concert Hall, still a major music venue. The wonderfully massive Bradford Odeon, which when it opened in 1930 was the third-largest cinema in Britain, is sadly being demolished.

A modern building just up the road houses the National Media Museum, the most visited museum outside London. In 2009 Bradford became the first-ever UNESCO City of Film.

Cathedral

Watching over the city centre from its lofty position on Church Bank is Bradford Cathedral, until 1919 the parish church of St Peter, and an unexpected gem. The main body of the church dates mostly from the 15th century, and the outside is businesslike, sporting a massive square tower with walls 11 ft (3.3 m) thick on which is fixed the first public clock in Bradford.

The interior of the cathedral is

gorgeous: a line of slender arches in rich creamy stone leads to a 20th-century east end by Sir Edward Maufe that shouldn't work but does – the modern lines blend seamlessly with the medieval and the whole effect is very satisfying. Brightly coloured angels, possibly from Kirkstall Abbey in Leeds, hold up the wooden roof, and among the memorials that decorate the old walls is a magnificent sculpture by John Flaxman, created in 1790 in memory of Abraham Balme (1706–96), a local businessman who was prominent in the development of Bradford. There is also a memorial plaque to the 56 people who died in the fire at Valley Parade football stadium in 1985.

Lister's Mill

The cathedral looks across the city centre toward another great Brad-

ford landmark, LISTER'S MILL, whose chimney, all 255 ft (78 m) of it, still dominates the city skyline. The mill was built in 1873 by SAMUEL CUNLIFFE LISTER (1815–1906), later Lord Masham, to replace his original Manningham Mill, which burned down in 1871. On its completion Lister's Mill employed 11,000 people and was THE BIGGEST TEXTILE MILL IN ENGLAND and THE LARGEST SILK MILL IN THE WORLD – the south shed alone is over ¼ mile (400 m) long.

The King of Velvet

The first weaver of wool was recorded in Bradford in 1241, but it was the industrial inventions of the 19th century that enabled Bradford to exploit to the full its plentiful natural resources of iron ore, coal and soft water. In 1800 the first steam-powered spinning mill opened, and by 1850 hand weaving had been replaced by power looms. However, it was Samuel Cunliffe Lister, born in Calverley Old Hall midway between Bradford and Leeds, who finally gave Bradford its edge over similar mill towns when he invented the LISTER NIP COMB, which for the first time made it possible to separate and straighten the raw wool mechanically, so that it was ready for being spun into yarn. By the 1860s Lister and Co had become THE FIRST TEXTILE COMPANY IN THE WORLD TO MECHANISE COMPLETELY THE MANUFACTURE OF SILK AND VELVET. Lister became the world's richest textile manufacturer and was known as the 'King of Velvet'.

Lister's Mill went on producing fabrics until 1992, including silk for parachutes during the Second World War, and supplied 1,000 yards (914 m) of velvet to Westminster Abbey for the Coronation of King George V in 1911 as well as velvet for the curtains in President Gerald Ford's White House in Washington DC in 1976. The mill has since been converted into luxury apartments.

A short walk from the mill is Lister Park, created out of the grounds of

Lister's home, the site of which is now occupied by an art gallery, the Cartwright Memorial Hall, named after Edmund Cartwright (1743–1823), inventor of the power loom.

Bolling Hall

Set in terraced gardens south of the city centre is Bradford's oldest house, the beautiful BOLLING HALL, home today to a museum of Bradford's history. It was begun as a fortified tower in the 14th century by Robert Bolling, and added to over the centuries, so that it is now a rambling mishmash of different periods from Tudor to Georgian.

In the 17th century Robert Bolling went out from here to Virginia, at the age of 14, and married Jane Rolfe, the granddaughter of Pocahontas. One of their descendants was Edith Bolling, second wife of US President Woodrow Wilson, and known as 'the first female President of the United States'.

BORN IN BRADFORD

FREDERICK DELIUS (1862–1934), composer.

WILLIAM JOWETT (1877–1965) and BENJAMIN JOWETT (1880–1963), manufacturers of Jowett cars in Bradford and Idle between 1906 and 1954.

J.B. PRIESTLEY (1894–1984), author, playwright (*Dangerous Corner, An Inspector Calls, Time and the Conways*) and founding member of the Campaign for Nuclear Disarmament. His ashes are scattered in the churchyard of the beautiful Norman church at Hubberholme in Upper Wharfedale.

MORRISONS, founded in 1899 by William Morrison, who began the business with an egg stall in Bradford's Rawson Market. By 2009 Morrisons was the fourth-largest supermarket chain in Britain.

ALBERT PIERREPOINT (1905–92), Britain's most prolific hangman. He executed over 400 people, including John Amery (1945), son of Secretary of State for India Leo Amery, for treason, William Joyce, Lord Haw Haw (1946), also for treason, serial killer John Christie (1953), and Ruth Ellis (1955), the last woman to be hanged in Britain.

RICHARD WHITELEY (1943–2005), presenter of *Countdown* and THE FIRST PERSON TO APPEAR ON CHANNEL 4, when it was launched in 1982.

KIMBERLEY WALSH (born 1981), singer with Girls Aloud.

Saltaire

Model Village

Built between 1852 and 1876, SALTAIRE WAS THE FIRST SUCCESSFUL LARGE-SCALE MODEL VILLAGE IN ENGLAND. The name Saltaire is derived from that of its founder, Sir Titus Salt, and of the River Aire beside which the mill sits.

Salt's Alpaca

TITUS SALT (1803–76) was born in Morley, near Leeds, the son of a successful wool-stapler. After joining his father's business, he learned the wool trade from the bottom up and took over the company in 1833. In

1836, on a visit to a wool supplier in Liverpool, Salt came across some unwanted bales of alpaca wool, which he purchased and proceeded to mix with sheep's wool and angora wool to make a hard-wearing worsted fabric he called alpaca. It became very fashionable and made his fortune.

In 1801 Bradford had a population of 13,000 and just one mill. By 1850 the population had risen to 104,000 and there were 129 mills, all pouring smoke into the air, and refuse and sewage into the little Bradford Beck, making Bradford the most polluted city in England. So, in 1850, Salt decided to build a new mill outside Bradford, on the enlightened basis that workers who were healthy and comfortable would work better and be more productive.

Salt's Mill

When SALT'S MILL opened in 1853, on 20 September to coincide with Salt's 50th birthday, it was THE BIGGEST AND MOST MODERN FACTORY IN EUROPE. Over the next ten years Salt built 850 homes for his workers, all with gas for heating and lighting, fresh water, and each with its own outside lavatory – unheard-of luxuries for those times. Saltaire also had its own church, shops, park, school, hospital and library – but no pub. Titus Salt was a member of the Congregational Church and was teetotal – which is why the name of the modern off-licence in Saltaire's main street is 'Don't Tell Titus'.

Sir Titus Salt is buried with members of his family in a mausoleum attached to Saltaire's sumptuous Italianate United Reform Church, which he had built in 1859.

Salt's Mill closed as a mill in 1986, and the following year was bought by Bradford-born business-man Jonathan Silver who converted it to mixed use. Today the mill houses light industries, shops, restaurants and a gallery showing THE LARGEST COLLECTION IN THE WORLD OF WORKS BY DAVID HOCK-NEY, born in Bradford in 1937.

In 2001 Saltaire was made a World Heritage Site.

Haworth

All about the Brontës

The desolate moorland village of HAWORTH, grey, cobbled and steep, is all about the Brontës, even though Charlotte, Emily, Anne and their brother Branwell were all born down the road in Bradford, in the small dining-room at No. 74 Market Street in Thornton, where their father was curate.

The family, father Patrick and his wife Maria and their six children, all came to live at the Parsonage in Haworth in 1820, and it was from here that the sisters would walk out on to the bleak moors that inspired their genius. Although Haworth has been partly industrialised since their day, the centre of the village is still unspoiled and atmospheric, especially when the mist comes down. A stiff climb up the high street leads into a small square, which contains a shop and the Black Bull Inn, where you can find the chair in which Branwell Brontë would sit and drink himself into a stupor. From the square a narrow lane leads to the church where the Brontës are buried in a family vault beneath the floor, all save for Anne who lies at Scarborough.

Looking down on the church from further up the lane, through a wooded graveyard, is THE PARSONAGE. It has been extended since the Brontës lived there, but is laid out inside as it was in their day, and is run by the Brontë Society as a museum. Without doubt this is one of the most imaginative and evocative museums in Britain, and as you wander through the house it almost seems possible that you might come across the Brontës talking or playing music, or hear the scratch of their pens. In the dining-room, where the girls did most of their writing, is the couch on which Emily died, aged just 30 – standing in that room it is impossible not to be moved.

Bleak Moors

The Parsonage sits right on the edge of the moors and marks the start of a number of walks that follow in the footsteps of the Brontë sisters, taking in such places as the Brontë Waterfall, 'a perfect torrent racing over the rocks, white and beautiful', and the Brontë Bridge nearby, which was replaced in 1990 after the original was washed away in a flood. There is also the Brontë Chair, a worn rock where

the girls would sit and write, and about 1 mile (1.6 km) beyond the waterfall, deeper into the moors, is Top Withens, the ruins of a farmhouse that is believed to have inspired Emily Brontë's *Wuthering Heights*. If the farmhouse itself did not, then certainly the location did – it is wild and dramatic even today.

Railway Children

The Brontë Parsonage appeared as Dr Forrest's surgery in the 1970 film of Edith Nesbit's *The Railway Children*, starring Jenny Agutter, which was filmed on and around the KEIGHLEY AND WORTH VALLEY RAILWAY. The railway, which follows the Worth valley for 5 miles (8 km) from Oxenhope to Keighley, is operated by volunteers, uses both steam trains and diesel, and is THE ONLY WHOLE, UNALTERED BRANCH LINE IN ENGLAND TO BE RUN AS A HERITAGE RAILWAY.

Mytholmes Tunnel between Haworth and Oakworth was the setting for the paper chase and landslide in the film, while Oakworth station was where Mr Perks the porter (played by Bernard Cribbins) was based, and where the children's father (Iain Cuthbertson) appeared out of the smoke and steam in the moving climax of the film. Mr Perks's cottage is by the level crossing at Oakworth station, and the children's house, called Three Chimneys in the film, is in fact Bent's Farm, located just above Oxenhope station. It is now a private home but can be seen from the public footpath through 'Top Field'.

East Riddlesden Hall

Bad Baronets

EAST RIDDLESDEN HALL is a wonderfully sinister 17th-century manor house that sits on a ridge above the River Aire, downstream from Keighley town centre. The stained black stonework and heavy, brutal architecture made it the perfect house to portray *Wuthering Heights* in the 1992 film of Emily Brontë's masterpiece starring Ralph Fiennes and Juliette Binoche.

East Riddlesden was built in 1642 by JAMES MURGATROYD, a rich cloth merchant from Halifax, and has remained virtually unchanged since then – a wing was added in 1692 but was demolished in 1905. Above the huge porch is a rose window thought to be the only one of its kind on a house in the West Riding.

Later members of the Murgatroyd family were renowned for their foul language and depravity, and local tradition has it that the River Aire changed course in disgust to avoid the house. W.S. Gilbert of Gilbert and Sullivan often stayed at East Riddlesden, and is said to have modelled the Bad (Murgatroyd)

Baronets of Ruddigore in his comic opera on these Murgatroyds.

Many of the rooms in the hall, and particularly what are now the tea rooms, are said to be haunted, with chairs and tables moving around and fresh flowers wilting overnight.

East Riddlesden Hall is now run by the National Trust and has been fitted out with 17th-century furniture to complement the original Murgatroyd panelling and plasterwork.

The Tudor twin-gabled stone tithe barn in the grounds is 120 ft (37 m) long, and ONE OF THE LARGEST TITHE BARNS IN ENGLAND.

Kirkstall Abbey

Industrial Beginnings

The massive ruins of KIRKSTALL ABBEY lie surrounded by green lawns beside the River Aire, some 3 miles (5 km) from the centre of Leeds. The abbey was founded in 1152 by Cistercian monks as a daughter house to Fountains Abbey, and is ONE OF THE MOST COMPLETE SETS OF MONASTERY RUINS IN ENGLAND.

By the end of the 12th century the monks had set up a corn mill on the river, the first stirrings of industry in the Leeds area, and after the monastery was dissolved in 1539 the mill complex developed into a major iron-producing forge, making KIRKSTALL FORGE ONE OF THE OLDEST INDUSTRIAL SITES IN BRITAIN as well as the cradle of Leeds's industrial development. It is currently undergoing redevelopment.

The ABBEY HOUSE MUSEUM, housed in the converted gatehouse of Kirkstall Abbey, is home to the HENRY COLLECTION, a compendium of prints, photographs and memorabilia about Victorian childhood that is unique.

Leeds

Industrial Capital of Yorkshire

LEEDS developed as a market centre for the Yorkshire woollen trade in the Middle Ages, and later exploited the iron-making and engineering skills of Kirkstall Forge to become the industrial capital of Yorkshire.

In 1792 James Watt installed one of his steam engines in Benjamin Gott's Bean Ings Mill in Wellington Street (now the site of the *Yorkshire Post*), and created THE FIRST FULLY AUTOMATED STEAM-POWERED WOOLLEN MILL IN THE WORLD.

Holbeck

As more wool merchants were attracted to Leeds as the centre of the wool trade, and as the advent of mechanisation meant that bigger mills were needed, entrepreneurs began to look for areas with space for them to develop. HOLBECK, a small weaver's village south of the town centre with a ready water supply, was perfect.

JOHN MARSHALL'S MILL was the first of the landmark factories to be constructed in Holbeck, and was THE BIGGEST MILL IN THE WORLD when it was opened in 1792.

In 1838 John Marshall commissioned another mill to be sited adjacent to his first. Designed by Ignatius Bonomi, TEMPLE WORKS was modelled on the Temple of Edfu in Horus, Egypt, and included a chimney resembling Cleopatra's Needle. The roof had 66 glass domes to let in light and ventilation, and was covered with grass to retain the humidity inside. The grass was kept tidy by a flock of grazing sheep. When it was created in 1840, Temple Works was THE LARGEST SINGLE ROOM IN THE WORLD.

The most distinctive features of the TOWER WORKS pin factory, erected in 1864, are the three towers which give the building its name. The largest and most ornate tower is styled on the Giotto campanile in Florence, the smaller ornate tower reflects Verona's

Lamberti Tower, and the most simple tower is similar to a Tuscan tower house.

All three factories are part of the HOLBECK URBAN VILLAGE, which is undergoing constant regeneration. One exhilarating approach to the area is through the Dark Arches underneath the City railway station, a long network of brick tunnels, once lined with shops, leading across the River Aire to Granary Wharf on the Leeds & Liverpool Canal. It is a nightmarish but thrilling experience to stand on the subterranean metal bridge across the river and watch the water gushing out from the cold, echoing blackness beneath the city centre.

Tetley's Brewery

Another vast enterprise south of the River Aire in Leeds is TETLEY'S BREWERY, founded in 1822 by Joshua Tetley and not long ago THE WORLD'S

BIGGEST PRODUCER OF CASK ALE. Tetley's was taken over by Carlsberg in 1998 and, despite huge protests, the Leeds brewery is to be closed in 2011 with production moved to Northampton.

City Centre

The wealth created by the factories is reflected in the many great Victorian buildings in the centre of Leeds, such as the vast, many-pillared TOWN HALL, opened by Queen Victoria in 1858 and ONE OF THE BIGGEST TOWN HALLS IN BRITAIN. The clock tower, 225 ft (69 m) high, serves as a symbol of Leeds. Charles Dickens came for the opening ceremony and stayed nearby at the SCARBOROUGH HOTEL, which stands on the site of the original, moated, LEEDS MANOR HOUSE, built in 1080.

Arcades

The Victorian shopping arcades in the centre of Leeds, GRAND ARCADE, THORNTONS ARCADE and COUNTY ARCADE, are regarded as THE FINEST VICTORIAN SHOPPING ARCADES IN BRITAIN. The VICTORIA QUARTER of interlinking arcades was designed by Frank Matcham, who usually designed sumptous theatre interiors, and his arcades are just as exuberant. In 1990 Queen Victoria Street was roofed over with THE LARGEST EXPANSE OF STAINED GLASS IN EUROPE, designed by Brian Clarke.

The Good Old Days

The LEEDS CITY VARIETIES MUSIC HALL is THE LONGEST CONTINUOUSLY RUNNING MUSIC HALL IN BRITAIN. It was built in 1865 by the landlord of the White Swan Inn as an entertainment area for his pub, and for 30 years between 1953 and 1983 it found nationwide fame as the home of the BBC television show *The Good Old Days*, compèred by Leonard Sachs, admired for his alliterative introductions. Approached along a rather scruffy alleyway, it all looks a bit run down from outside, but the interior is gorgeous, and the whole theatre is undergoing refurbishment, due to be completed in 2011.

Some Leeds Pioneers

Matthew Murray
(1765–1826)

Born in Newcastle, MATTHEW MURRAY opened a factory in Holbeck in 1795 to produce the flax-spinning machines he had invented. This was developed into THE WORLD'S FIRST STEAM ENGINEERING FOUNDRY, for making another of Murray's inventions, a commercially viable steam engine. The ROUND FOUNDRY, as it became known, was THE FIRST SITE IN LEEDS TO HAVE GAS LIGHTING, and Murray's own house nearby used steam piped across from the foundry to provide heating. Known as Steam Hall, it was ONE OF THE FIRST CENTRALLY HEATED HOUSES IN ENGLAND.

In 1812 Murray supplied the Middleton Railway in the south of the city with his twin-cylinder Salamanca steam locomotive. This was an improved version of a design by Richard Trevithick (to whom Murray paid a royalty) and proved to be THE WORLD'S FIRST COMMERCIALLY SUCCESSFUL STEAM LOCOMOTIVE.

The MIDDLETON RAILWAY in Leeds was established in 1758 by THE FIRST-EVER RAILWAY ACT OF PARLIAMENT, and is HENCE THE OLDEST CONTINUOUSLY WORKING RAILWAY IN THE WORLD. Built to carry coal from the Middleton Colliery to the centre of Leeds, it was originally a horse-drawn wooden wagon-way, but in 1810 the manager of the colliery, John Blenkinsop, seeking to carry greater loads, relaid one side of the track with a toothed rail designed to mesh with a suitably adapted steam locomotive, thus inventing THE WORLD'S FIRST RACK RAILWAY. To run on it he purchased a steam locomotive called Salamanca, manufactured by Matthew Murray at the Round Foundry in Holbeck. This was THE FIRST STEAM ENGINE EVER BUILT WITH TWO CYLINDERS, and in 1812 became THE FIRST STEAM LOCOMOTIVE EVER TO OPERATE PROFITABLY. In 1960 the Middleton Railway was THE FIRST STANDARD-GAUGE RAILWAY TO BE TAKEN OVER BY A PRESERVATION SOCIETY and today runs passenger services over 1 mile (1.6 km) of track between Hunslet and Middleton Park.

Joseph Hepworth
(1834–1911)

Born in Huddersfield, JOSEPH HEPWORTH opened a tailoring business on Wellington Street in Leeds in 1864, which rapidly grew to employ 500 people, making mainly three-piece suits. In 1880 Hepworth opened his first shop to sell directly to the public, and within ten years had over 100 retail outlets. By the 1920s, Joseph Hepworth & Son had become THE BIGGEST CLOTHING MANUFACTURER IN BRITAIN.

In 1981 Hepworth's bought Kendall's rainwear shops in order to develop a chain of shops for women under the name of Next. Over the following few years Next for Men and Next Interiors were introduced, and in 1986 Hepworth's changed its name to Next plc, which is how it is known today.

Michael Marks
(1859–1907)

Born in Slonim in Russian-controlled Poland, MICHAEL MARKS came to England while in his 20s, to escape the persecution of Jewish people. With no job and unable to speak much English, he made his way to Leeds, where he had been told there was a company run by SIR JOHN BARRAN, THE INVENTOR OF 'OFF THE PEG' CLOTHING, that employed Jewish refugees. He was taken on by a ware-house owner called Isaac Dewhurst to sell Dewhurst goods in the communities around Leeds, and proved to be so good at selling that he made enough money to set up his own stall in Leeds's Kirkgate market, under a sign that read 'Don't ask the price. It's a penny'.

More stalls followed, and in 1894 Marks went into partnership with Isaac Dewhurst's cashier THOMAS SPENCER, who invested £300 in the business, and so Marks & Spencer was born. Michael Marks's son Simon introduced the 'St Michael' brand name in the 1930s in honour of his father. In 1984 a clock was placed in Kirkgate market on the site of Marks's first stall to celebrate the centenary of its opening.

Joseph Aspdin
(1788–1855)

Born in Hunslett, the son of a bricklayer, JOSEPH ASPDIN invented THE FIRST ARTIFICIAL CEMENT by burning together clay and ground limestone.

As the result was the colour of Portland stone, Aspdin decided to call it PORTLAND CEMENT. It was a considerable improvement on the first modern concrete cement, which had been invented in Leeds in 1756 by another native of the city, JOHN SMEATON (1724–92), known as THE FIRST CIVIL ENGINEER. He had used powdered brick and pebbles.

Joseph's son, WILLIAM ASPDIN, born in Leeds in 1815, set up a cement works in Rotherhithe in London in 1841. He supplied Portland cement to Marc Isambard Brunel for use in THE WORLD'S FIRST UNDERWATER TUNNEL, THE THAMES TUNNEL, which thus became THE FIRST MAJOR CIVIL ENGINEERING PROJECT IN THE WORLD TO USE CEMENT. The cement company started by William Aspdin eventually became BLUE CIRCLE, which at one time was THE LARGEST CEMENT MANUFACTURER IN THE WORLD.

First on Film

French photographer LOUIS AIMÉ AUGUSTIN LE PRINCE (1842–90), a designer at Whitley Partners, his wife's family's engineering firm, made Leeds the star of THE VERY FIRST MOVING PICTURES THE WORLD HAD EVER SEEN. In early October 1888, using a single-lens camera he had designed at his workshop in Woodhouse Lane, he

filmed members of the Whitley family in the garden of his father-in-law Joseph's house, in Oakwood Grange Road, Roundhay. The film can be dated prior to 24 October 1888, because Le Prince's mother-in-law Sarah, who appears in the film, died on 24 October . Also featured in the film are Joseph Whitley, a Miss Harriet Hartley and Le Prince's eldest son – all immortalised as THE FIRST HUMAN BEINGS TO APPEAR IN MOVING PICTURES.

Later that same month, from a second-floor window of Hicks Bros, ironmongers, Le Prince filmed the moving traffic on LEEDS BRIDGE – now immortalised as THE FIRST BRIDGE IN THE WORLD TO APPEAR IN MOVING PICTURES.

Not long afterwards, Le Prince and all his equipment disappeared from a train in France, never to be seen again. The mystery of what happened to the man regarded as the true 'Father of Motion Pictures' has never been solved.

Well, I never knew this
about
AIREDALE

MALHAM TARN, where the River Aire rises, is THE HIGHEST LAKE IN ENGLAND at 1,240 ft (378 m) above sea level. The clergyman novelist CHARLES KINGSLEY would often come and stay with his friend Walter Morrison at TARN HOUSE on the north shore of the lake, and the local scenery inspired his book *The Water Babies*. The red-faced squire in the book, John Hartover, was based on his host.

ALL HALLOWS, BARDSEY, has what is possibly THE EARLIEST SAXON CHURCH TOWER IN BRITAIN. The lower half of the tower was originally built as a porch some time before AD 950, and then added to later in the same century. Just down the road from the church is THE BINGLEY ARMS, originally the Priests Arms, which has a strong claim to being THE OLDEST PUB IN BRITAIN. The church records of 905 speak of a Priests Inn, and this could have been a rest house for the workmen who were building the church.

Across the river from Saltaire is the SHIPLEY GLEN CABLE TRAMWAY, which climbs for ¼ mile (400 m) through the woods of Shipley Glen. Opened in 1895, it is THE OLDEST WORKING CABLE TRAMWAY IN BRITAIN.

The PARSONAGE AT HAWORTH was bought in 1928 by SIR JAMES ROBERTS, a native of Haworth who was by then the owner of Salt's Mill, at Saltaire, where he had worked as a boy. He donated the house to the Brontë Society to run as a museum.

On display in the CLIFFE CASTLE MUSEUM in KEIGHLEY is the loom of TIMMY FEATHER, THE LAST WEAVER TO USE A HAND-LOOM IN ENGLAND. Baptised by Patrick Brontë in 1825, Timmy lived and worked in a cottage in Stanbury, and would carry his cloth across the moors to the Piece Hall in Halifax. He died in 1910.

IDLE, a suburb of Bradford, was the home of JOWETT CARS from 1946 until 1954. Membership of the IDLE WORKING MEN'S CLUB, which brings with it the prestigious Idle Working Men's Pass, is internationally sought after, and honorary members include Roger Moore, Mohamed Al Fayed and Lester Piggot. The club logo is of a workman leaning on a shovel.

The church at ADEL, on the northern outskirts of Leeds, is ONE OF THE MOST COMPLETE NORMAN CHURCHES IN ENGLAND, and is especially renowned for its fantastically carved south doorway and sanctuary door knocker – the present one is only a replica, as the original was stolen.

WETHERBY racecourse is THE ONLY RACECOURSE IN YORKSHIRE TO HOST JUMP RACING EXCLUSIVELY.

LEEDS CARNIVAL, first held in 1967, is THE OLDEST WEST INDIAN CARNIVAL IN EUROPE, and THE SECOND LARGEST IN BRITAIN after London's Notting Hill Carnival.

SKY PLAZA in Leeds is THE TALLEST STUDENT ACCOMMODATION BLOCK IN THE WORLD, at 338 ft (103 m).

HENRY, LORD DARNLEY (1545–67), second husband of Mary Queen of Scots and father of James I, was born at TEMPLE NEWSAM, a superb Tudor and Jacobean pile that is probably the oldest big house in Leeds. Henry VIII gave Temple Newsam to Darnley's parents, the Earl and Countess of Lennox, after executing the former owner Sir Philip Darcy for his part in the Pilgrimage of Grace. In 1922 Lord Halifax donated the house to Leeds Corporation, who now run it as a splendid museum. In the grounds, which were laid out by Capability Brown, is THE LARGEST WORKING RARE BREEDS FARM IN EUROPE.

HERBERT HENRY ASQUITH (1852–1928), Liberal Prime Minister from 1908 to 1916, was born in MORLEY, the son of a wool merchant. During his time in office the controversial 'People's Budget' was put together by his Chancellor of the Exchequer, Lloyd George, introducing National Insurance and pensions. As Prime Minister for the first two years of the First World War, Asquith was held partly responsible for the disasters of Gallipoli and the Somme, where his son Raymond died. He also had to deal with the Easter Rising in Ireland. His second wife Margot Tennant was a celebrated wit, and his enjoyment of a glass or two attracted the nickname of 'Squiffy' – a word created especially for him referring to both his name and to the description 'skew-whiff', which is apparently how he stood at the Dispatch Box. When, on his retirement, he became the Earl of Oxford and Asquith, the noted wag Lady Salisbury remarked that it was like 'a suburban villa calling itself Versailles'.

HENRY MOORE (1898–1986), Britain's most influential sculptor of the 20th century, was born in CASTLEFORD.

ERNIE WISE (1925–99), comedian and one half of much-loved comedy duo Morecambe and Wise, was born Eric Wiseman in BRAMLEY, Leeds. In 1985, on 1 January, he made THE FIRST MOBILE PHONE CALL IN BRITAIN, on the Vodaphone network, from St Katharine's Dock in London to Vodaphone's head office in Newbury.

The peerless author, actor and playwright ALAN BENNETT was born in ARMLEY, Leeds, in 1934. Perhaps his best-known works are the plays *The Madness of George III* and *The History Boys*, both of which he adapted for the cinema. In 1996 he turned down a knighthood.

ALFRED AUSTIN (1835–1913), THE FIRST JOURNALIST TO BECOME POET LAUREATE, was born in HEADINGLEY.

HEADINGLEY is now headquarters of YORKSHIRE COUNTY CRICKET CLUB, which in 1992 became THE LAST COUNTY CLUB IN ENGLISH CRICKET TO DROP THE RULE THAT ITS PLAYERS MUST HAVE BEEN BORN WITHIN THE COUNTY BORDERS.

ARTHUR RANSOME (1884–1967), author of *Swallows and Amazons*, was born in HYDE PARK, Headingley, at No. 6 Ash Grove. There is a blue plaque on the house. Singer CORINNE BAILEY RAE was born in Leeds and lived in the Hyde Park area.

One of the few remaining picture palaces, the HYDE PARK PICTURE HOUSE, which opened in 1914, still has much of the original interior, including an ornate Edwardian balcony. It is THE ONLY GAS-LIT CINEMA STILL IN USE IN BRITAIN.

DON VALLEY

Chapel of our Lady of Rotherham Bridge, the best-preserved of the surviving bridge chapels in England

Sheffield

The Dawn

It was in fields alongside the RIVER SHEAF, nearly 1,200 years ago, that both Sheffield and England were born. The Sheaf then formed part of the boundary between the Saxon kingdoms of Mercia and Northumbria, and in 829 at Dore, some 5 miles (8 km) to the south-west of modern Sheffield's city centre, King Eanred of Northumbria kneeled in submission to King Egbert of Wessex, acknowledging Egbert as the first King of all Saxon England. A stone on the green at Dore marks the moment.

Across the River Sheaf from DORE is a small church attached to a great stone tower, all that is left of THE ONLY PREMONSTRATENSIAN ABBEY IN THE WEST RIDING, BEAUCHIEF ABBEY, founded in 1175. The monks from the abbey created a small mill and forge down by the river, which later developed into a full-blown steelworks that operated until the 1930s. ABBEYDALE

HAMLET, as it is known, is now run as one of Sheffield's principal industrial heritage museums.

Beauchief Abbey

At about the same time as the abbey was put up, or a little earlier, the Normans built a castle and a church downstream where the Sheaf meets the River Don, to protect and monitor the communities that were springing up in the hills around – like Rome, Sheffield is built on seven hills. The castle is long gone, destroyed by the Civil War, its memory kept alive only

by street names and Castle Square. The church is now Sheffield Cathedral.

Cutlery

Wood from the valleys, iron ore from the hills, and power from the rivers gave rise to industry in Sheffield as long ago as the 13th century. The first record of a cutler in Sheffield comes from 1297, with the tax records of one Robert the Cutler. One hundred years later Chaucer, in his *Canterbury Tales*, tells of a 'Sheffield thwitel', or knife, in the 'hose' of the Miller of Trumpington. By the 1600s, three in every five Sheffield men were cutlers and in 1624, in the reign of James I, a trade guild for the metalworkers of Sheffield was established, known as the COMPANY OF CUTLERS IN HALLAMSHIRE. Headed by the Master Cutler, it still promotes and supports all the industries of Sheffield today from the grand Cutlers' Hall of 1832, which stands opposite the cathedral.

In 1773, fed up with having to send its silverware to London for hall-marking, Sheffield got together with Birmingham to petition for their own assay offices. The petitioners met up in London at the Crown and Anchor inn, and when they got their own hall-marks, Sheffield chose a crown, while Birmingham went for an anchor. Later, a Yorkshire Rose was chosen as the hallmark for Sheffield gold. Today, SHEFFIELD'S ASSAY OFFICE IS THE BUSIEST IN BRITAIN.

'Through all Europe we're known;
To the Indies our goods go,
Through Afric' they're shown;
Likewise through the American coast
The cutlers of Sheffield their
commerce can boast.'
Sheffield song (1780)

City of Steel

What really propelled Sheffield to world fame as the City of Steel, which by the 1860s was producing 50 per cent of all the steel used in Europe and 90 per cent of the steel used in Britain, was the entrepreneurial and inventive genius of a small number of brilliant men.

Benjamin Huntsman
(1704–76)

BENJAMIN HUNTSMAN was a Quaker toolmaker and steel manufacturer from Lincolnshire, who settled at Handsworth in Sheffield in the 1740s to take advantage of cheaper fuel for his furnaces. As a precision craftsman, he found himself hampered by poor quality steel, and so set about devising ways to improve it. He learned from the local glassmakers how to create extremely high temperatures by burning coke rather than charcoal, and these temperatures enabled him to melt raw steel to produce cast ingots of high and uniform quality steel. To contain the hot steel he designed a crucible made from clay that could withstand the high temperatures, and the resulting product became known as 'crucible' steel (a name reflected in Sheffield's Crucible Theatre, home of the World Snooker Championships).

The cutlers in Sheffield were wary of crucible steel at first because it was hard to work, so Huntsman sold his entire output to the French, and they soon began to threaten Sheffield's dominance by making products that were of a far superior quality. Sheffield responded by sending one of their own, an iron-founder called Walker, to infiltrate Huntsman's works in Handsworth, disguised as a beggar seeking shelter by the fire. Walker learned the secret of the process, which Huntsman had failed to patent, and reported back to his colleagues, who quickly began to make their own crucible steel, rekindling Sheffield's rise to prominence.

Thomas Boulsover
(1705–88)

THOMAS BOULSOVER was born in Sheffield and set up as a cutler in the city centre. In 1743, while repairing the handle of a silver and copper decorative knife, he over-heated it so that the silver began to melt and then stick to the copper. Further experiments revealed that a thin layer of silver on top of a thick layer of copper could be fused together by heat and then shaped, and in this way it was possible to produce items that looked like solid silver but could be made at a fraction of the cost. Thomas Boulsover had invented SHEFFIELD PLATE, which brought silver goods into the reach of many more people – and made Boulsover, and Sheffield, very rich.

John Brown
(1816–96)

In 1860 JOHN BROWN became THE FIRST STEEL MANUFACTURER IN THE WORLD TO OBTAIN A LICENCE TO USE A NEW, HOT-AIR PROCESS OF STEEL MAKING, DEVELOPED BY HENRY BESSEMER. This process was able to produce much larger quantities of refined steel than the crucible method and Brown was soon able to supply huge numbers of steel rails for the expanding railway industry, as well as armour plating for the ships of the

Royal Navy. Sheffield's place as Britain's main steel producer was further enhanced.

Harry Brearley
(1871–1948)

HARRY BREARLEY was born in Sheffield and became a research assistant at Firth's, a local steel company. In 1912 while trying to find a way to stop rifle barrels from rusting, he discovered that by mixing steel with chromium in certain proportions he could produce an alloy that was much more resistant to corrosion than ordinary steel. Harry Brearley had invented STAINLESS STEEL, which is still widely used for a whole range of items today.

Turret House

Sheffield does possess some history other than just steel. Mary Queen of Scots was held prisoner in Sheffield as a guest of the Earl of Shrewsbury, who by then had moved from the old castle to Sheffield Manor, a more comfortable home in the castle grounds. The

manor is now just a ruin in what is now Norfolk Park, but a small detached stone building nearby, known as the TURRET HOUSE, remains intact. It is thought that this was built especially for Mary, and you can still appreciate the splendid plaster ceilings and climb the spiral staircase to the roof, where the Queen took the air and admired the extensive views, which are somewhat different today.

First for Football

• SHEFFIELD FOOTBALL CLUB (Sheffield FC) was founded in 1857 and is THE OLDEST CLUB IN THE WORLD NOW PLAYING ASSOCIATION FOOTBALL.

• In 1860 SHEFFIELD FC played THE FIRST INTER-CLUB FOOTBALL MATCH IN THE WORLD, against nearby HALLAM, which was founded in 1860 and is THE SECOND-OLDEST FOOTBALL CLUB IN THE WORLD. The game was held at Hallam's SANDYGATE ROAD stadium, where Hallam still play, and which is consequently THE OLDEST FOOT-BALL GROUND IN THE WORLD.

• Sheffield FC and Hallam still meet for this 'Sheffield' derby match, which is THE OLDEST FOOTBALL DERBY IN THE WORLD.

• In 1867 Hallam won the association football YOUDAN CUP, sponsored by local theatre owner Thomas Youdan, and THE FIRST ORGANISED FOOT-BALL TOURNAMENT IN THE WORLD. The game was played at the BRAMALL LANE STADIUM, home of Sheffield United Cricket Club, THE FIRST ENGLISH SPORTS CLUB TO USE THE TERM UNITED IN ITS NAME. Football was first played at Bramall Lane in 1862, and it is now THE OLDEST MAJOR STADIUM IN THE WORLD WHERE PROFESSIONAL FOOTBALL IS STILL PLAYED. In 1878 Bramall Lane hosted THE WORLD'S FIRST-EVER FLOOD-LIT FOOTBALL MATCH, between two teams from the Sheffield Football

Association. Today Bramall Lane is home to Sheffield United, the football club formed by Sheffield United Cricket Club in 1889.

• Bramall Lane was the first headquarters of the Yorkshire County Cricket Club before it moved to Headingley in 1893.

• One of the clubs who used Bramall Lane was the WEDNESDAY CRICKET CLUB, so named after the day of the week on which they played their matches. In 1867, at a meeting in the Adelphi Hotel, now the site of the Crucible Theatre, the club decided to establish a football team for the purpose of keeping the players fit during the winter. The football team was known as the Wednesday Football Club, and it quickly became one of the leading teams of the day and turned professional. In 1899 the club moved to a new ground at Hillsborough, and in 1929 changed their name to SHEFFIELD WEDNESDAY. In 1989 one of the worst football tragedies of all time occurred at Hillsborough, when 96 Liverpool fans were crushed to death as too many people were squeezed into one section of the ground for an FA Cup semi-final match.

Rotherham

Church and Chantry

ROTHERHAM is dominated by the huge Rotherham Minster, which sits on a high mound at the centre of the town and sports a very satisfying spire, 180 ft (55 m) high. Church and spire are 15th century, and the minster is regarded as one of the finest examples of medieval Perpendicular architecture in England.

The church is a rare treasure to find in what is a somewhat rundown place, and another gem is the handsome 15th-century BRIDGE CHAPEL which stands on the old four-arched bridge across the Don, ONE OF ONLY FOUR SURVIVING BRIDGE CHAPELS IN ENGLAND. The old bridge is now for pedestrians only and a new bridge for traffic runs alongside.

Rotherham Plough

In the 18th and 19th centuries Rotherham had a thriving iron industry. In 1730 JOSEPH FOLJAMBE invented an improved design of plough, using iron fittings, which became known as the 'ROTHERHAM' PLOUGH. Although it was not the first iron plough, it was the first that was commercially successful, and was light enough to be drawn by a pair of horses. The Rotherham plough remained the standard plough in Britain for 180 years until the introduction of the tractor.

Rotherham foundries also produced cannon for the Royal Navy, including those used at the Battle of Trafalgar by HMS *Victory*, and in 1854 Samuel Beale & Co produced the wrought-iron plates for the biggest ship in the world, Isambard Kingdom Brunel's SS *Great Eastern*.

Rotherham is the birthplace of two of England's finest goalkeepers, GORDON BANKS, born in 1937 at Tinsley, on the south-west edge of the town, and DAVID SEAMAN, born in 1963.

Joseph Bramah
(1748–1814)

JOSEPH BRAMAH, engineer and inventor known as the 'Father of Hydraulic Engineering', was born in the village of WENTWORTH between Barnsley and Rotherham.

His first invention, in 1778, was an improved WATER CLOSET, which used a hinged flap at the bottom of the bowl to stop the water from freezing. This proved very successful and durable, and one of Bramah's original water closets is still in use at Osborne House, Queen Victoria's holiday home on the Isle of Wight.

Next came a new LOCK MECHANISM, patented in 1784, which was so secure that Bramah put an example in the window of his shop in London's Piccadilly and offered a reward of 200 guineas to anyone who could pick it. It was almost 70 years before the prize was won. An American, A.C. Hobbs, who was visiting the Great Exhibition in Hyde Park, laboured for 52 hours over 16 days before successfully opening the lock – although his methods remain controversial to this day. The 'CHALLENGE LOCK', as it became known, was rebuilt and can be seen in the Science Museum.

Bramah's greatest invention was the HYDRAULIC PRESS, for which he was granted a patent in 1795, and which is named in his honour as the BRAMAH PRESS. Along with William Armstrong, Bramah was the first and most important pioneer of hydraulic engineering, and his ideas are still used by the modern hydraulic industry everywhere.

Wentworth Woodhouse

Europe's Longest Façade

WENTWORTH WOODHOUSE, near Rotherham, was built in the 1730s by THOMAS WATSON-WENTWORTH, later 1ST MARQUESS OF ROCKINGHAM, and has THE LONGEST FAÇADE OF ANY HOUSE IN EUROPE, 606 ft (185 m) long, making the house twice as wide as Buckingham Palace. The house is so vast that nobody has ever found out how many rooms there are – most people lose count at about 250. In its heyday guests were issued with coloured confetti to drop in their wake so that they could find their way back to the main part of the house from their bedrooms.

In the 1300s the Wentworths had married into the Woodhouse family, hence the double-barrelled name, which is strangely appropriate because Wentworth Woodhouse is, to all intents and purposes, two houses, one facing west, the other east. The brick west front was built in modest baroque style in 1725 to replace the old Jacobean house of Thomas Wentworth, 1st Earl of Strafford, who was beheaded for

treason in 1641. The east front, which has the massively long façade, was made so stupendous in order to irritate the other branch of the Wentworths, who were at the time building themselves what was intended to be the biggest house in Yorkshire, at Wentworth Castle near Barnsley.

In 1751 Wentworth Woodhouse was inherited from his father by the 2nd Marquess of Rockingham, who served as Prime Minister twice.

Fitzwilliams

The 2nd Marquess died childless and Wentworth Woodhouse passed to his nephew, the 4th Earl Fitzwilliam, who commissioned Humphrey Repton to lay out a formal garden in keeping with the magnificence of the house.

William, the oldest son of the 6th Earl Fitzwilliam, was born with epilepsy, which in those days was considered a form of madness, and he was sent to Canada to be kept out of sight. While he was there he made a pioneering trek across Canada from the east coast to the west, becoming THE FIRST EUROPEAN TO CROSS THE YELLOWHEAD PASS IN THE ROCKY MOUNTAINS. He later wrote about his

adventures in a book called *The North-West Passage by Land*, which was well received in England, and he came home to win a seat as one of the youngest MPs at Westminster.

William predeceased his father and so Wentworth Woodhouse was inherited, amidst some controversy, by the 6th Earl's grandson, also William, but known as Billy. Billy had been born in the wilds of Canada, and some of the Fitzwilliams claimed that he was a changeling, inserted in place of the real child, either to rid the bloodline of epilepsy or because the real child was a girl, who would not be able to inherit for that branch of the family.

Nonetheless Billy did inherit, becoming the 7th Earl Fitzwilliam, and a popular figure in Yorkshire. In 1909 he built a motor-car factory on his land at Tinsley in Sheffield, which produced the SHEFFIELD SIMPLEX, a luxury car to rival the Rolls-Royce. The company survived until 1925, the very last car being made for Earl Fitzwilliam himself.

Manny's Revenge

Billy died in 1943, having been a much-loved landlord who treated his staff and workers well, but leaving his son Peter, the 8th Earl, to face the challenge of the new post-war Labour government. MANNY SHINWELL, a left-wing Glasgow MP who was Minister of Fuel and Power, ordered the digging up of the park and gardens at Wentworth Woodhouse, 'right to the back door', ostensibly to extract coal needed to power the railways in the aftermath of the war. In reality the coal was of poor quality and the scheme was an excuse to destroy the Fitzwilliams, whom Shinwell saw as a prime example of the 'privileged rich'. Despite pleas to the Prime Minister Clement Atlee from the estate workers, who protested that the Fitzwilliams were admired in Yorkshire and had always been generous employers, Shinwell was unbending and the grounds at Wentworth Woodhouse, including a glorious beech avenue, were dug up and turned into the LARGEST OPEN-CAST MINE IN BRITAIN. Mining continued until the 1950s, and the grounds have since returned to their natural state, but the woodland and formal gardens were lost for ever.

The 8th Earl Fitzwilliam, a war hero who fought with the Special Operations Executive (SOE) and was awarded a DSO, died in a plane crash over France during a storm in 1948.

With him in the plane was the sister of the future US President John F. Kennedy, KATHLEEN KENNEDY, with whom the Earl had been having an affair. She was killed as well.

During the next few years the contents of Wentworth Woodhouse were sold or transferred to other Fitzwilliam properties, and the larger part of the house was leased out to the local council and Sheffield Polytechnic. The last member of the family to live there was the 10th Earl, who died in 1979. The whole house was then briefly let to a businessman who went bankrupt, and the present owner of the lease is a reclusive architect called CLIFFORD NEWBOLD, who is rarely seen.

The glorious east front of Wentworth Woodhouse can, however, always be seen from the TransPennine Way which runs alongside the grounds. It is an unforgettable sight, especially when illuminated by the rays of the rising sun.

Conisbrough

Oldest Round Keep

The great white circular keep of CONISBROUGH CASTLE, standing on a ridge above the small town of Conisbrough, is THE OLDEST ROUND KEEP IN ENGLAND. Built in 1185 by Hameline Plantagenet, the man responsible for raising Richard I's ransom, it is 90 ft (27 m) high, has six massive buttresses, and looks almost new. The keep is entered via a very small doorway and along a narrow passage through the walls, which are 15 ft (4.6 m) thick. Stone steps lead past circular rooms to the roof, from which there is a breathtaking view of four counties.

About two-thirds of the way up, on the third floor, is a tiny and quite lovely oratory, built into one of the buttresses. Only about 12 ft (3.6 m) long, it nonetheless has peepholes, a vaulted roof and a good deep arch.

One of our most remarkable ancient places, the chapel is full of atmosphere, which plainly impressed Sir Walter Scott, for he made Conisbrough the castle of the Saxon kings and the chapel the setting for a dramatic scene in his novel *Ivanhoe.* The castle is now run by the Ivanhoe Trust, for English Heritage.

Often overlooked, as much by the visitor as by the castle, is Conisbrough's ancient church of St Peter, which was originally a Saxon church, enlarged by Hameline Plantagenet at the time he was putting up the castle. Although much has been added over the centuries there is still plenty of Norman work left, including the tower and a deep chancel arch. The most striking possession is a huge Norman gravestone, lavishly carved with figures, including Adam and Eve under a tree, a knightly tournament, and a man fighting a dragon.

Well, I never knew this
about
THE DON VALLEY

SIR FRANCIS CHANTREY (1782–1841), regarded by many as England's greatest sculptor, was born, and is buried, in the village of NORTON, now a suburb of Sheffield. His sculpture of the tragic *Sleeping Children* in Lichfield Cathedral is one of the most sublime works of art in England. For some years Chantrey had a studio in Sheffield's PARADISE SQUARE, the city's only remaining Georgian square, and something of a gathering place, where John Wesley and Rowland Hill preached and the Chartists held rallies. In the chancel of the cathedral perched above the square is Chantrey's first commission in marble, a bust of James Wilkinson, vicar there for 50 years.

Monty Python's MICHAEL PALIN was born in Sheffield in 1943, as was THE FIRST BRITON IN SPACE, HELEN SHARMAN, in 1963. She flew to the *Mir* space station aboard the Soviet *Soyuz TM12* space capsule in 1991. Actor Sean Bean was born in HANDSWORTH in 1959.

Sheffield boasts THE LARGEST ARTIFICIAL SKI RESORT IN EUROPE.

Pilgrim Father WILLIAM BRADFORD (1590–1657) was born in the Manor House at AUSTERFIELD, near Doncaster, and was baptised there in the simple Norman church of St Helen's. He became a member of the Brownists, an extreme Separatist group of Puritans, and sailed in the *Mayflower* to the New World in 1620 to escape the persecution of James I. He was elected Governor of Plymouth Colony five times, and the Society of Mayflower Descendants helped restore the church in Austerfield in honour of 'the first American citizen of the English race who bore rule by the free choice of his brethren'.

Among the descendants of William Bradford are the Doubledays publishing family, George Eastman, founder of Eastman Kodak, Dr Spock the child care specialist, Noah Webster of Webster's Dictionary and actors Clint Eastwood, Christopher Reeve, John Lithgow and the Baldwin brothers, Alan, Daniel, William and Stephen.

BARNSLEY, which sits in the middle of the Yorkshire coalfield, ONCE THE BIGGEST COALFIELD IN BRITAIN, is the

birthplace in 1938 of ARTHUR SCARGILL, former President of the National Union of Mineworkers and founder of the Socialist Labour Party. He led the Miners' Strike of 1984–5.

Barnsley is also the birthplace of comedian HARRY WORTH (1917–89), legendary cricket umpire HAROLD 'DICKIE' BIRD, born in 1933, and TV chat show host MICHAEL PARKINSON, born in 1935.

Harry Worth performing his party trick

DONCASTER is the home of THE WORLD'S OLDEST CLASSIC HORSE RACE, THE ST LEGER, named after its founder, Lieutenant-Colonel Anthony St Leger. Established as a two-mile race for three-year-olds, it was first run on 24 September 1776, over Doncaster's Cantley Common, and moved to its present home, Turf Moor, in 1779. The St Leger is THE LONGEST OF THE FIVE ENGLISH CLASSICS and has only been cancelled once in its history, in 1939 at the outbreak of the Second World War.

GUISELEY, near Leeds, is home to THE BIGGEST AND MOST FAMOUS FISH AND CHIP SHOP IN THE WORLD, HARRY RAMSDEN'S. Harry began serving his battered fish and chips, made to a secret recipe, in 1928, from a striped wooden hut beside a tram stop by the busy White Cross junction. Within three years he was able to open his fish and chip 'palace' on the same site, decorated with Ritz-style chandeliers and oak panelling. The palace seats 250 and serves up to a million customers a year. Although Harry Ramsden's outlets can now be found all over the world, Guiseley remains the spiritual home of the company – and the striped hut where it all began is still in its same place beside the main restaurant.

HARRY CORBETT (1918–89), creator of the glove puppet Sooty, was Harry Ramsden's nephew, and from time to time would play the piano in his uncle's fish and chip shop. Corbett, who was born in Bradford, grew up in Guiseley where his parents owned their own fish and chip shop called SPRINGFIELD FISHERIES – it is still there.

ST OSWALD'S PARISH CHURCH IN GUISELEY was used by many generations of the Longfellow family, and the grandfather of the American poet HENRY LONGFELLOW left for America from there in the 18th century. In 1812 the parents of the Brontë sisters, PATRICK BRONTË from Ireland and MARIA BRANWELL from Penzance, were married in St Oswald's.

Kirklees and the Calder Valley

Wakefield Cathedral, with Yorkshire's tallest spire

Wakefield

Capital

WAKEFIELD is the capital of the West Riding and of the Metropolitan County of West Yorkshire. It became the centre of Yorkshire's woollen industry in Norman times, and remained the centre until the Industrial Revolution, when the trade moved to Bradford and Leeds.

Wakefield's mainly 14th-century cathedral stands on the site of a Saxon church right at the heart of the city, atop a small green hillock by the Bull Ring shopping centre. Unlike most cathedrals it is not protected from the everyday bustle and business of the city by a close, and so feels very much part of the community, with people dropping in from their offices or while out shopping. The 15th-century spire was restored by George Gilbert Scott and, at 247 ft (75 m) high, is THE TALLEST SPIRE IN YORKSHIRE.

Oldest Bridge Chapel

Spanning the River Calder nearby is a long, nine-arched bridge, nearly 700 years old, which is adorned by Wakefield's great treasure, the medieval CHANTRY CHAPEL OF ST MARY, built during the Black Death around 1350, and THE OLDEST AND MOST ORNATE OF THE FOUR BRIDGE CHAPELS LEFT IN ENGLAND. In 1847 the glorious west front was removed and taken to Kettlethorpe Hall, 3 miles (5 km) south of Wakefield, where it now forms the façade of an ornamental boathouse. A new west front, modelled closely on the original, was created by George Gilbert Scott, unfortunately out of soft Caen stone, and this in turn had to be replaced in 1939 by a façade made from hard gritstone.

Mystery Plays

Wakefield is also known for the WAKEFIELD MYSTERY CYCLE, a collection of 32 medieval plays based on the Bible that chart Mankind's journey from the Creation to the Final Judgement, and were originally performed in the churches and streets of Wakefield around Corpus Christi day. The manuscript of the Wakefield cycle, written in the 15th century by an anonymous author known as the Wakefield Master, is considered the best of the four surviving full cycles (York, Wakefield, Chester and the oddly named 'N' Town). The Wakefield Mystery Plays are revived from time to time today and performed at various venues around Yorkshire.

Rhubarb

Wakefield is the capital of the RHUBARB TRIANGLE, an area of roughly 9 sq miles (23 sq km) around Wakefield, where not so long ago OVER 90 PER CENT OF THE WORLD'S FORCED RHUBARB WAS GROWN. In honour of this the city hosts an annual Rhubarb Festival in February.

BORN IN WAKEFIELD

JOHN RADCLIFFE (1652–1714), physician to William and Mary, who gave his name to Oxford's Radcliffe Infirmary, Radcliffe Observatory and Radcliffe Camera (which originally housed the Radcliffe Science Library).

JOHN HARRISON (1693–1776), clockmaker, born at FOULBY. Harrison invented the marine chronometer, which helped to solve the problem of establishing longitude while at sea.

JOHN CARR (1723–1807), architect known as John Carr of York, responsible in Yorkshire for Harewood House and Constable Burton Hall, as well as much of Wentworth Woodhouse and Aske Hall.

DAME BARBARA HEPWORTH (1903–75), modernist sculptor. She died in a fire at her studio in St Ives, Cornwall, where she had created an outdoor theatre for her sculptures in the garden. Many of her sculptures are on display at the new Hepworth Wakefield gallery, opened in 2010.

Nostell Priory

Paine and Adam

NOSTELL PRIORY was begun in 1735, on the site of the 12th-century priory of St Oswald, for SIR ROWLAND WINN, 4th baronet, from a family of London textile merchants who had bought the estate in 1650. Plans were originally drawn up by a local architect named Colonel James Moyser, but these were taken over and modified in 1736 by a rising young architectural star called JAMES PAINE, who was just 19 years old at that time, and who would continue to be associated with Nostell Priory for the next 30 years.

Only the main block was finished when Sir Rowland Winn, 5th baronet, inherited the estate in 1765, and he commissioned the most fashionable designer of the day, Paine's rival ROBERT ADAM, to complete the interior and to add four pavilions to the house. Alas, only one had been completed, along with a new double staircase for the front of the main house, when the 5th baronet died in a road accident in 1785, and work came to a halt, leaving the house with a somewhat lopsided appearance. The contrast between the Paine and the Adam parts of the house makes a fascinating study. The rooms that Robert Adam designed at Nostell Priory are considered to be amongst the best examples of his work anywhere.

Chippendale Collection

Nostell Priory also boasts THE MOST COMPREHENSIVE AND BEST-DOCUMENTED COLLECTION OF CHIPPENDALE FURNITURE IN THE WORLD – rivalled only by that at Harewood House. Much of the furniture sports the Winn family crest, and it was all designed and built especially for Nostell Priory by THOMAS CHIPPENDALE himself, who was born nearby at OTLEY in 1718 – the site of his birthplace is marked by a blue plaque. Chippendale is also thought to have made the exquisite doll's house, with all its miniature furniture and figures, which can be seen in the Museum Room at Nostell Priory.

Another treasure of the house is a longcase clock made by JOHN HARRISON, also a local man (*see* above), in 1717.

Although the Winn family, made Barons St Oswald in 1885, still have the use of an apartment in the Adam wing of Nostell Priory, the entire estate of over 300 acres (120 ha) now belongs to the National Trust, making it ONE OF THE LARGEST PROPERTIES OWNED BY THE NATIONAL TRUST.

Pontefract

Liquorice Town

PONTEFRACT grew up not just around a broken bridge, as its name suggests, but also around a castle and a priory. The priory has completely disappeared, but the remains of the castle are still visible, scattered about a rocky hill above the rooftops of the town. Reached by a steep, uneven, stone stairway, much of the site had been made into a garden. The most noticeable remnant is the unusual Round Tower or donjon, similar to that of Clifford's Tower in York.

PONTEFRACT CASTLE was built in 1070, and was later described by Oliver Cromwell as 'one of the strongest inland garrisons in the kingdom'. John of Gaunt made Pontefract his home, and of the many famous prisoners held at Pontefract over the years perhaps the most tragic was Richard II, last of the Plantagenets, sent here by Gaunt's son Henry Bolingbroke (later Henry IV), in 1400, and left to starve. Also incarcerated in the castle were James I of Scotland and Charles, Duke of Orleans, author of the first Valentine's card, who was captured at the Battle of Agincourt in 1415.

Good Enough to Eat

Pontefract Castle appears on the product for which Pontefract is most famous, the PONTEFRACT CAKE, a small disc of liquorice shaped like a coin. Liquorice plants were first brought to Pontefract from the Middle East by the Cluniac monks of Pontefract Priory during the time of the Crusades. They used liquorice for medicinal purposes, and the deep loamy soil around Pontefract made it one of the very few places in England where the plant could thrive. In 1760 a local chemist, George Dunhill, decided to add sugar and make liquorice sweets, and Pontefract's reputation as England's Liquorice Town was established.

Liquorice is no longer grown in Pontefract, but there are still two producers of Pontefract cakes in the town: Haribo, who took over Dunhills, and Tangerine Confectionery, once Monkhills, who make the Sherbert Fountain with its famous liquorice straw.

Huddersfield

Splendid

HUDDERSFIELD RAILWAY STATION has been described as a stately home with trains in it. It was designed by James Pigott Pritchett and built between 1846 and 1850, and John Betjeman thought it had 'the most splendid station façade in England'.

The station faces on to St George's Square, where there is a bronze statue of the late Prime Minister SIR HAROLD WILSON (1916–95), who was born in Huddersfield.

Others who were born in Huddersfield include the actor JAMES MASON (1909–84) and the businessman LORD

Liquorice made in Pontefract has starred in a number of films.

- In the 1925 film *The Gold Rush*, Charlie Chaplin is seen eating his boots and laces, all made out of liquorice from Pontefract.
- A 1949 film called *Adam's Rib*, starring Katharine Hepburn and Spencer Tracy, featured a scene with a liquorice gun made in Pontefract.
- On London Weekend Television's 1950s programme *Beat the Clock* Acker Bilk played 'Stranger on the Shore' on a clarinet made from Pontefract liquorice.
- In the 1979 James Bond film *Moonraker*, starring Roger Moore, the character called Jaws is seen biting through an electric cable, which was in fact purpose-made in Pontefract from liquorice.

Huddersfield station

HANSON (1922–2004), founder of Hanson plc.

TETLEY TEA began life as Tetley Brothers in Huddersfield in 1837. It was founded by JOSEPH AND EDWARD TETLEY, who started by peddling salt and then tea from a packhorse on the Yorkshire Moors. In 1953 Tetley INTRODUCED THE TEA BAG INTO BRITAIN, 33 years after it had been invented in America.

DAVID BROWN LTD was founded in Huddersfield in 1860, making patterns for cast gears. By the 1920s they had become THE LARGEST MANUFACTURER OF WORM GEARS IN THE WORLD. In 1936 they went into tractor manufacture, firstly in partnership with Harry Ferguson, with whom they produced THE WORLD'S FIRST HYDRAULIC LIFT TRACTOR, and then on their own, taking over the silk mill of Jonas Brook and Brothers at Meltham on the edge of Huddersfield, where they produced tractors from 1939 until 1988. In 1947 the then managing director David Brown (1904–93), who was born in Huddersfield, acquired the carmaker ASTON MARTIN and went on to build the legendary 'DB' series, including the DB5 driven by James Bond in *Goldfinger*.

Huddersfield was THE BIRTHPLACE OF RUGBY LEAGUE, in 1895, when representatives of 20 northern rugby clubs met at the George Hotel and agreed to resign from the Rugby Football Union and form the Northern Rugby Football Union, which went on to become the Rugby Football League.

Kirklees

Robin Hood

'Here underneath dis laitl stean
Laz robert earl of Huntintun
Ne'er arcir ver as hie sa geud
An pipl kauld im robin heud
Sick utlawz as his as iz men
Vil england nivr si agen
Obiit 24 kal: Dekembris, 1247.'

So reads the inscription on the gravestone of ROBIN HOOD, lost deep in the thick woods of the Kirklees estate on the edge of Mirfield, just north of Huddersfield.

The story goes that Robin Hood, towards the end of his life, came to Kirklees Priory to be tended by the Prioress, his cousin, little knowing that she was in league with his arch-enemy Sir Roger of Doncaster. In the pretence of healing him, the Prioress bled Robin so severely that he was fatally weakened. Little John arrived when Robin was almost spent and helped him to a window, where Robin shot a last arrow from his trusty bow, asking that he should be buried where the arrow landed. And that is where he lies to this day. The grave is almost impossible to find, being on a private estate and far from any public foot-paths. Nonetheless it is protected by iron railings from souvenir hunters, many of whom believe that fragments from the grave can cure illness.

Kirklees Priory

KIRKLEES PRIORY was founded in 1155 during the reign of Henry II, but was dismantled by Henry VIII at the Disso-lution of the Monasteries in 1539, and the stone used to build Kirklees Hall on the same site. All that remains of the priory is the tiny priory guesthouse nearby, where Robin Hood is said to have died, although it cannot have been in this actual building, which only dates from the 15th century. The guest-

house is in a state of near collapse and needs urgent attention, but it sits on private land and nothing can be done without the consent of the owners. Robin's grave is some 700 yards (640 m) from the guesthouse, a mighty distance for even a fully fit Robin Hood to send an arrow.

Make It So

The actor SIR PATRICK STEWART, most widely known for his role as Jean-Luc Picard, captain of the starship *Enter-prise*, in the TV series *Star Trek: The Next Generation*, was born at No. 17 Camm Lane in MIRFIELD in 1940, and as a boy appeared in pantomime at the local church.

Halifax

Hell, Hull and Halifax

HALIFAX is a handsome town that rises out of a deep vale in the Pennines and has been a centre of the woollen trade since the 15th century. Until the mid

17th century theft of cloth was punishable with beheading by the Halifax Gibbet, a kind of guillotine, which stood in Gibbet Street. This harsh law gave rise to the Beggar's Litany, 'From Hell, Hull and Halifax, good Lord deliver us!'

HALIFAX MINSTER, dedicated to St John the Baptist, dates from the 12th century. In 1766 WILLIAM HERSCHEL, who would go on to discover the planet Uranus, became the church's first organist.

Bits and Pieces

The magnificent HALIFAX PIECE HALL, opened in 1779, is THE ONLY SURVIVING MANUFACTURERS' HALL IN BRITAIN. Called the Piece Hall because it was where weavers took their 'pieces', or lengths of cloth to be sold, it consists of a huge central courtyard surrounded on four sides by classical colonnaded galleries that shelter over 300 merchant's shops. Since the Piece Hall was restored in 1976 these shops have housed speciality shops, galleries, restaurants, a museum and exhibition space. Concerts and flea markets are held in the courtyard, which today acts as Halifax's central square.

DEAN CLOUGH MILLS, which fills the valley floor on the north side of Halifax, was built in the 1840s for CROSSLEY'S CARPETS and was once THE LARGEST CARPET MILL IN THE WORLD, over ²⁄₃ mile (1.1 km) long. Closed for carpet production in 1938, it is now a flourishing business park.

The HALIFAX BUILDING SOCIETY was founded in 1853 and was once THE BIGGEST BUILDING SOCIETY IN THE WORLD. In 1973 the Halifax took possession of its new headquarters, an awesomely modern concrete-and-glass, diamond-shaped building at the top of the town, built over computerised fireproof vaults. In 2001 the Halifax merged with the Bank of Scotland and became the Halifax Bank of Scotland or HBOS, which in turn was taken over by the Lloyds Banking Group after the credit crunch of 2008. Halifax is still the headquarters of the Halifax portion of Lloyds HBOS.

World's Tallest Folly

Perched on the edge of a precipice high above the town is Halifax's most astonishing landmark, the WAINHOUSE TOWER, which at 275 ft (84 m) high, is THE TALLEST FOLLY IN THE WORLD. It was originally built in 1875 as a chimney to carry away smoke from John Wainhouse's dye works, but when the factory was sold and the new owner refused to use the chimney, Wainhouse decided to make it a thing of beauty and use it as an observatory. The worryingly slender tower was restored in 2006, but only rarely is it open for the public to essay the long climb of 403 steps to the viewing platform at the top, from where the views must be stupendous – and dizzying.

Toffee Town

In 1890 JOHN MACKINTOSH (1868–1920) and his new bride Violet opened a confectionery and pastry shop in Kings Cross Lane in Halifax. They wanted to have a speciality product that would make a name for their shop, and decided to try combining soft American caramel with brittle English butterscotch to produce a high-quality toffee. Mackintosh's toffee proved so popular that it soon outsold everything else in the shop, and in 1899 they had to move to bigger premises in Queens Road. John Mackintosh became known as the 'TOFFEE KING' and Halifax the 'TOFFEE TOWN'. Although Mackin-

tosh's merged with Rowntree's and was eventually taken over by Nestlé, their most popular brand, Quality Street, introduced in 1936, is still made in Halifax.

Percy Shaw
(1890–1976)

PERCY SHAW, the eccentric inventor of the CAT'S EYE, was born in Halifax. Shaw came up with the idea for cat's eyes after he was driving home from the pub on a foggy night when his headlights were reflected in the eyes of a cat sitting at the side of the carriageway, a stroke of luck which prevented him from driving off the road. He decided to try and replicate this effect, and in 1934 patented his invention which consisted of two spheres of reflective glass set in a rubber casing within a cast-iron housing. As traffic passes over the structure it sinks into the road and the glass is cleaned by water retained in the base. Shaw called his invention a cat's eye in honour of the cat that had saved him – although in another version he said he got the idea for a reflective device after using the polished tramlines in Bradford to navigate in the dark.

Cat's eyes proved particularly useful during Second World War blackouts, and in 1947 the Minister for Transport James Callaghan adopted them for use along Britain's main roads. They were eventually sold across the world and Percy Shaw became one of the richest men in Britain, although he never moved from the home in Halifax where his parents had moved to when he was two. He stripped the house of carpets and curtains and lived in a huge bare room with just three televisions, permanently switched on for company.

Holmfirth

Tinsel Town

Nestling in a deep valley where the rivers Home and Ribble meet, HOLM-FIRTH is a pleasing bustle of stone cottages and shops that jostle for space on the steep Pennine slopes. It looks like the archetypal Dales village, but Holmfirth also has much in common with Hollywood, and not just its name – 'holm' is Old British for holly while 'firth' is Old English for wood. In the early 1900s, thanks to a local man called JAMES BAMFORTH, born in Cartworth in 1842, Holmfirth rivalled or indeed surpassed Hollywood in terms of film production and innovation.

Bamforth started his professional life as a studio photographer in 1870, and some ten years later progressed to making magic lantern slides at his studio in Station Road in Holmfirth. This enterprise proved so successful that Bamforth had to extend his studio to keep up with demand. He specialised in life model slide sequences, photographed in front of a painted backdrop, and used friends and members of his own family as his subjects. His experience in the field led to him being asked in 1898 to create a number of films for a Bradford firm of film equipment makers to show their customers. Over the next couple of years he produced some 15 short films, including some of the world's first narrative films.

Bamforth's 1899 release *The Kiss in the Tunnel* contains THE FIRST KNOWN EXAMPLE OF FILM EDITING. A later film, *Ladies' Skirts Nailed to a Fence*, features THE EARLIEST KNOWN EXAMPLE OF A CONTINUITY CUT.

Postcards

From 1902 Bamforth began to concentrate on postcards, with his sons, while after a short break the Holmfirth Studios started to produce films under a director called Cecil Birch. After the First World War Birch and the new Holmfirth Producing Company moved to London, and the last film made in Holmfirth was *Meg o' the Woods*, which came out in 1918.

Bamforth's now began to use artists' drawings for their postcards instead of real models, and developed the style of 'saucy' postcards for which they are most fondly remembered today. The postcards were produced well into the 1990s and until not long ago many examples were on display in the Postcard Museum housed in the Picturedrome. Now, alas, the museum collection has gone and it is almost impossible to find a Bamforth saucy postcard anywhere in the town where they were made. The Bamforth Studio in Station Road has been converted into flats.

Sid's Cafe

The PICTUREDROME, originally called the Holme Valley Theatre, opened in March 1913, making it ONE OF THE OLDEST CINEMAS IN BRITAIN. It is still used as an entertainment venue today.

Summer Wine

Holmfirth is now famous as the home of Compo, Foggy and Clegg from the BBC's *Last of the Summer Wine,* THE LONGEST-RUNNING TV SITUATION COMEDY IN THE WORLD, first aired in 1973. Many of the locations used in the show are instantly recognisable. NORA BATTY'S HOUSE, where she was usually found sweeping the steps or beating Compo with her broom, can be seen from the Upper Bridge, while SID'S CAFÉ, where they all regularly meet for a cup of tea, is tucked away in the square beneath the church – and on non-filming days is open to the public for teas, snacks and souvenirs.

Well, I never knew this
about

KIRKLEES AND THE CALDER VALLEY

WALTON HALL near Wakefield, now a hotel, was the birthplace and ancestral home of the eccentric naturalist CHARLES WATERTON (1783–1865), one of THE WORLD'S FIRST ENVIRONMENTALISTS. He travelled widely throughout South America, collecting together unusual animals and plants to bring back to Yorkshire. In order to preserve them he invented a novel type of taxidermy, soaking the specimens in mercuric chloride and then arranging them into lifelike poses, sometimes as grotesque caricatures of real people. Many of his stuffed animals have survived and are on display in Wakefield Museum. They are extraordinarily lifelike. On returning from his travels, Waterton enclosed 250 acres (100 ha) of the Walton Hall estate inside a 9 ft (2.7 m) high wall that ran for 3 miles (4.8 km), and created THE FIRST WILDFOWL AND NATURE RESERVE IN THE WORLD. In one of THE FIRST ENVIRONMENTAL CAMPAIGNS he later challenged a nearby soap works that was polluting the park and succeeded in having it fined and moved on.

SANDAL CASTLE was a 12th-century motte and bailey castle on a high mound on the edge of Wakefield. In 1460, during the Wars of the Roses, Richard Duke of York gathered his army of some 8,000 to 10,000 men on top of the mound in preparation for attacking a superior Lancastrian force that was surrounding him. He eventually led his men down the hill to engage the enemy in what became the Battle of Wakefield. His actions are thought to be the origin of the children's nursery rhyme 'The Grand Old Duke of York':

> 'The grand old Duke of York,
> He had ten thousand men;
> He marched them up
> to the top of the hill,
> And he marched them down again.'

MARTIN FROBISHER (1535–94), seaman and explorer, was born in ALTOFTS, near Pontefract. He made three voyages in search of the North West Passage and was THE FIRST EUROPEAN TO SEE WHAT BECAME KNOWN AS BAFFIN ISLAND, where Frobisher Bay is named after him. He was knighted for his role in the defeat of the Spanish Armada.

ALTOFTS once possessed THE LONGEST ROW OF TERRACED HOUSES IN EUROPE,

SILKSTONE ROW, built in 1865 for miners from the West Riding Colliery. The colliery closed in 1966 and Silkstone Row was demolished in 1974.

WAKEFIELD was the location OF BRITAIN'S FIRST OPEN PRISON, opened in 1936.

SHIBDEN HALL, the loveliest house in Halifax, sits in glorious isolation on the other side of a hill from the town, in the midst of delightful gardens with terraces, rock gardens and a boating lake. It was built in 1420, came into the hands of the Listers in 1612 and was eventually inherited and restored by ANNE LISTER in 1826. Anne Lister (1791–1840) is often referred to as THE FIRST MODERN LESBIAN, as she lived openly with her lover Ann Walker and penned a series of cryptic diaries chronicling her affairs. She was also a great traveller and adventurer, becoming THE FIRST WOMAN TO CLIMB TWO OF THE HIGHEST MOUNTAINS IN THE PYRENEES, MONT PERDU and the VIGNEMALE. Shibden Hall is now run by Halifax Council as a museum.

HOLMFIRTH ARTWEEK IS THE BIGGEST PUBLIC ENTRY ART EXHIBITION IN ENGLAND.

ROGER HARGREAVES (1935–88), author of the *Mr Men* series of children's books, was born in CLECKHEATON, north of Huddersfield.

The SUMMIT TUNNEL, which takes the Manchester–Leeds railway underneath the Pennines near Todmorden, is one of the oldest railway tunnels in the world. When it opened in 1841, it was THE LONGEST TUNNEL IN THE WORLD at 1.6 miles (2.57 km) long.

The octagonal Methodist chapel in HEPTONSTALL, near Hebden Bridge, was founded in 1764, and is THE OLDEST SURVIVING OCTAGONAL METHODIST CHAPEL STILL IN CONTINUOUS USE IN THE WORLD.

Buried in the new churchyard of St Thomas à Becket at Heptonstall is the American poet SYLVIA PLATH, who was married to poet laureate TED HUGHES, born in the nearby village of MYTHOLMROYD. Plath's headstone, which reads Sylvia Plath Hughes, is frequently vandalised by people trying to chip the name Hughes off the stone – they blame Hughes for Plath's suicide.

PONTEFRACT has one of the most beautiful racecourses in England. It winds amongst trees and parkland for 2 miles and 125 yards (3.35 km), and is THE LONGEST CONTINUOUS RACECOURSE IN EUROPE.

The best view of Huddersfield is from the VICTORIA TOWER, perched on CASTLE HILL, just south of the town. The tower was built in 1899 to celebrate Queen Victoria's Diamond Jubilee and provides some of the most spectacular views in Yorkshire. Annoyingly, the tower is only open on a limited number of days each year.

The television and radio transmitter on ELMLEY MOOR, south-east of Huddersfield, is 1,084 feet (330 m) high and THE TALLEST FREE-STANDING STRUCTURE IN BRITAIN.

West Riding Dales and the Ouse

*Selby Abbey, the first monastery to be founded
in the North after the Norman conquest*

Skipton

Cliffords

Skipton Castle, much of which
survives from Norman days, is one of
the best-preserved castles in England,
largely thanks to the redoubtable
Lady Anne Clifford, only surviving child of George Clifford, 3rd Earl
of Cumberland. She made it her life's
work to restore and refurbish all the

Clifford properties which were scattered about the North, and to mark
the completion of the work at Skipton in 1659 she planted a yew tree in
the lovely little central courtyard.
Skipton Castle was originally given
by Edward II to Robert Clifford, from
the same family

as Henry II's mistress the Fair Rosamund Clifford, in 1310. Robert later lost his life at the Battle of Bannockburn in 1314.

THOMAS SPENCER (1852–1905), co-founder of Marks & Spencer, was born in Skipton. Also born in Skipton, at Clifford House, was IAN MACLEOD (1913–70), Conservative Chancellor of the Exchequer, and the man who coined the word 'stagflation'.

Ilkley

Therapy

The SPAW BATHS, now called WHITE WELLS, which look down on Ilkley from Ilkley Moor, opened in 1843 and formed THE FIRST HYDROPATHIC SPA FOR THE COLD WATER CURE IN BRITAIN. CHARLES DARWIN took the treatment there in 1859, the year his book *On the Origin of Species* was published.

ILKLEY GOLF CLUB is THE THIRD OLDEST GOLF CLUB IN YORKSHIRE, and was where Britain's most successful Ryder Cup player, COLIN MONTGOMERIE, learned his golfing skills. Former Ryder Cup captain MARK JAMES, who lives in Ilkley, is an honorary life member. SIR EDWARD MAUFE (1883–1974), the architect of Guildford Cathedral, was born in Ilkley, as was gardener and television presenter ALAN TITCHMARSH, in 1949.

Walk west out of Ilkley and climb Heber's Ghyll to find THE ONLY SWASTIKA STONE IN BRITAIN, a boulder on which some prehistoric man has carved a cross like a swastika – what it signifies is a mystery.

Knaresborough

Fugitives and Apothecaries

KNARESBOROUGH is a picturesque old town situated in a deep gorge formed by the River Nidd, with the ruins of a Norman castle perched high above it. An early constable of the castle was HUGH DE MORVILLE, one of the four knights who murdered Thomas à Becket in Canterbury Cathedral. After they had committed their dastardly deed the knights hid in Knaresborough Castle for three years. The view from the castle, over the roofs of the old grey houses that tumble down to the river, and across the splendid, towering railway viaduct to the church, is exhilarating.

In the market square stands THE OLDEST CHEMIST SHOP IN BRITAIN, which began trading as a pharmacy in 1720 when John Beckwith was the apothecary. Today the lovely old brick house is occupied by a tea-room.

Mother Shipton

'Carriages without horses shall go
And accidents fill the world with woe
Around the world thoughts shall fly
In the twinkling of an eye
Iron in the water shall float
As easy as a wooden boat
Gold shall be found
In a land not now known.'

So spake MOTHER SHIPTON, born in a cave across the River Nidd from Knaresborough in 1488, amidst thunder and lightning and her dying mother's screams. Her real name was URSULA SOUTHEIL, she married a local man despite being hideously ugly, and she came to be regarded as England's most celebrated prophetess, apparently foretelling, amongst other things, the defeat of the Spanish Armada in 1588 and the Great Fire of London in 1666. The cave where she was born is reached by a pleasant walk along the river through the trees.

England's Oldest Tourist Attraction

Next to Mother Shipton's cave is ENGLAND'S OLDEST TOURIST ATTRAC-

TION, THE PETRIFYING WELL, which opened its gates in 1630. Fed by a spring that has never been known to dry up, a silver curtain of water flows down an overhanging rock face into a huge bowl resembling a giant's face. The water is laced with minerals, and any item that is placed in the rock pool becomes covered with mineral deposits, which slowly harden, making it appear as though the object has turned to stone. Strung across the rock face are a variety of petrified objects that people have brought to the well over the years, such as teddy bears, gloves and hats.

The well is located in an old royal forest that was sold by Charles I to Sir Charles Slingsby in 1630. Sir Charles wanted to exploit all the visitors who came to see Mother Shipton's Cave, and so he fenced off the well and charged people to look at it – no one had thought of doing such a thing before.

There is another cave by the river, not far away, where a hermit named ROBERT FLOWER lived in the 12th century. It is now known as ST ROBERT'S CHAPEL. Next to it is the extraordinary HOUSE IN THE ROCK, a good-sized dwelling place carved into the rock face by Thomas Hill, a linen weaver, in the 1770s. Although lived in by the descendants of Thomas Hill, the House in the Rock, also known as Fort Montague, has always been run as a tourist attraction.

Harrogate

Royal Hall Theatre

Yorkshire's Spa

In 1571 SIR WILLIAM SLINGSBY of Knaresborough took a drink from a spring on the other side of the River Nidd and noticed that the water tasted like the medicinal waters of Spa in Belgium. The word spread and Harrogate was on its way to becoming one of the most fashionable spa towns in Europe. The site of the original well, in the delightful open spaces of THE STRAY, is covered by a pillared dome.

Harrogate's heyday was in the 19th and early 20th centuries, and hence most of the architecture in the town is Victorian or Edwardian. The ROYAL BATHS were THE LARGEST HYDROTHER-APY ESTABLISHMENT IN THE WORLD when they opened in 1897. The ROYAL HALL THEATRE, created by Frank Matcham in 1903, is BRITAIN'S ONLY SURVIVING KURSAAL, or 'cure hall', designed as an entertainment venue for those taking the waters.

After the First World War Harro-gate's popularity as a spa declined, but during the Second World War the town's big hotels were used to accommodate government ministries evacuated from London, and this led to Harrogate's development as a premier conference centre. HARRO-GATE INTERNATIONAL CENTRE opened in 1982 and in that same year hosted the EUROVISION SONG CONTEST.

In 1895 a Harrogate doctor, DR PRITCHARD ROBERTS, became THE FIRST DOCTOR IN BRITAIN TO USE A CAR FOR DOING HIS ROUNDS, in this case a Benz.

Two much-loved Harrogate enter-prises are BETTYS TEA ROOMS, who opened their first tea-room in Harro-gate in 1919, and TAYLORS OF HARROGATE, who produce YORKSHIRE TEA and are one of the few remain-ing family tea merchants in Britain. The two companies merged in 1962.

In December 1926, Harrogate became the focus of media attention when the crime writer AGATHA CHRISTIE was discovered staying at the OLD SWAN HOTEL under the name of her husband's mistress, Theresa Neele. She had disappeared from her home in Surrey 11 days earlier, sparking off one of the biggest manhunts in British history.

Harrogate was the birthplace of CRIMPLENE, a material developed by ICI in the 1950s and named after Crimple valley, south of the town, where the factory was located.

Selby

One of Yorkshire's Three Great Churches

SELBY is one of the few provincial towns in England that have given a king to England – in this case HENRY I, William the Conqueror's youngest and only English-born son, who was born in Selby in 1068. William and his wife Matilda were staying in the town while the King was attempting to sort out the North after the Conquest.

In 1069 William granted a charter to a French monk from Auxerre called Benedict to establish an abbey at Selby. Benedict had been told in a dream that he should build a church in England at a place where he saw three swans land on the water – those three swans now form the official crest of the abbey. Selby was the first monastery to be founded in the North of England after the Norman Conquest, and survived the Dissolu-

tion of the Monasteries by becoming the parish church – it is THE ONLY MONASTIC CHURCH IN YORKSHIRE TO HAVE SURVIVED AS A PARISH CHURCH almost intact.

The abbot who came after Benedict was called Hugh and he replaced Benedict's wooden church with one of stone, much of which survives today, including the tower. The main entrance to the abbey is through the 12th-century West Doorway, which is one of the finest examples of Norman architecture in the country. Inside, on the south side of the nave, is HUGH's PILLAR, decorated with a diamond pattern similar to one of the pillars in Durham Cathedral, where Hugh was trained. Opposite are a number of amazingly distorted arches, a result of the foundations of the tower sinking in the 12th century.

Built into the wall of the north choir aisle is a squint hole used by lepers to watch services from outside the abbey. There is also a hollow capital on top of one of the pillars inside which is an exquisite carved portrait of Edward VII – it can be seen with the use of the torch provided.

The greatest architectural treasure of Selby Abbey is the East Window, known as the JESSE WINDOW as it depicts the family tree of the Kings of Israel from Jesse of Bethlehem to Mary and Jesus. Created in about 1330, the window is considered a masterpiece of Decorated tracery and stained glass, most of which survived a great fire in 1906 because the wind changed direction just in time.

Another famous window, and a feature that brings a great many Americans to Selby, is the 15th-century WASHINGTON WINDOW, high up in the south clerestory of the choir. Picked out in medieval glass are three red stars above two red bands upon a shield, the earliest known depiction of the heraldic arms of the Washington family, ancestors of the first President of the United States. The American flag, the Stars and Stripes, is based on the shield in this window, which was given to the abbey to commemorate George Washington's distinguished ancestor John Wessington, Prior of Durham (1371–1451).

during the Wars of the Roses, the BATTLE OF TOWTON WAS THE LARGEST AND BLOODIEST BATTLE IN BRITISH HISTORY. Up to 90,000 men took part, 50,000 on the Lancastrian side and 40,000 on the Yorkist side, and there were some 28,000 casualties. Victory went to the Yorkists, led by Edward IV, and although the result was not decisive there were some years of uneasy peace afterwards.

An obelisk stands by the road on the spot where the Lancastrian leader LORD DACRE is said to have fallen, shot by a boy hiding in the branches of a tree. He is buried in the churchyard at nearby Saxton, beneath an impressive chest tomb, an unusual treasure to find in so small a country churchyard.

Other victims are thought to be buried beneath the grassy fields that surround YORKSHIRE'S SMALLEST CHURCH, ST MARY'S CHAPEL AT LEAD, just along the road to the west of Saxton. It stands all alone beside the River Cock, which was said to run red with blood after the battle.

St Mary's was built in the 12th century as a chapel for a vanished manor

The Battle Of Towton

Britain's Bloodiest Battle

Fought on snowy windswept fields above the village of Towton, east of Leeds, on Palm Sunday in 1461

house next door, and contains the graves of several members of the Tyas family, occupants of the manor. There is also a three-decker pulpit and a Norman font. The church was saved from ruin by a group of ramblers in 1931, and is now cared for by the Church Conservation Trust and is always open.

Well, I never knew this about

THE WEST RIDING DALES AND THE OUSE

The YORKSHIRE DALES NATIONAL PARK is THE LARGEST AREA OF LIMESTONE LANDSCAPE IN BRITAIN.

The SETTLE–CARLISLE RAILWAY, opened in 1876, is England's most scenic railway and RIBBLEHEAD VIADUCT is the biggest and longest viaduct on the railway. Built between 1870 and 1875, Ribblehead has 24 arches, is 104 ft (32 m) high and ¼ mile (400 m) long. A little to the north is the longest tunnel on the railway, the BLEA MOOR TUNNEL, 2,629 yards (2,404 m) in length and completed in 1874. DENT RAILWAY STATION, between Dent and Cowgill, stands at 1,150 ft (351 m) above sea level and is THE HIGHEST RAILWAY STATION ON ENGLAND'S NATIONAL RAILWAY NETWORK.

The main chamber of GAPING GILL, a giant cave on the flanks of Ingleborough Hill, is THE BIGGEST KNOWN CAVE CHAMBER IN BRITAIN. Fell Beck disappears inside, creating ENGLAND'S HIGHEST UNBROKEN WATERFALL, which plunges into the void for 360 ft (110 m).

WHITE SCAR CAVE under Ingleborough Hill is THE LONGEST SHOW

CAVE IN BRITAIN, covering just over 1 mile (1.6 km).

On top of INGLEBOROUGH HILL are the remains of THE HIGHEST IRON AGE FORT IN BRITAIN, 2,373 ft (723 m) above sea level.

THE WORST LOSS OF LIFE IN BRITISH CAVING HISTORY occurred beneath the Yorkshire Dales in June 1967, when six young cavers (the oldest was 26) were drowned in the MOSSDALE CAVERNS on the eastern flank of Wharfedale. Their bodies were at first left in the cave where they died, but were later moved to a higher cavern called the Sanctuary where they now rest undisturbed – the system was permanently sealed off to prevent further tragedy.

In 1963 the STUMP CROSS CAVERNS near Pateley Bridge were the scene of a world record, when GEOFF WORK-MAN remained underground there for 105 days, as part of an experiment to see how the human body would react to being deprived of the natural day and night cycle.

THE OLDE SWEET SHOP in PATELEY BRIDGE, established in 1827, is THE OLDEST SWEET SHOP IN ENGLAND.

At CAUTLEY SPOUT, near Sedbergh, the Red Gill Beck tumbles 650 ft (199 m) in a long series of waterfalls which form THE LONGEST WATERFALL ABOVE GROUND IN ENGLAND.

GOOLE is ENGLAND'S FARTHEST INLAND PORT, 50 miles (80 km) from the sea. It has two distinctive water towers, known as 'the salt and pepper pots'. The red brick 'pepper' tower was built in 1885 and held 30,000 gallons, but soon proved to be too small and was replaced in 1927 by the reinforced concrete 'salt' tower, 145 ft (44 m) high, holding 750,000 gallons. At the time of its construction the 'salt' tower was THE BIGGEST WATER TOWER IN EUROPE.

DRAX POWER STATION is THE LARGEST AND NEWEST COAL-FIRED POWER STATION IN BRITAIN.

Gazetteer

York and Ripon

Jorvik Viking Centre

Coppergate, York, YO1 9WT
Tel: 01904 543400
www.jorvik-viking-centre.co.uk

Clifford's Tower, York

Tower Street, York, YO1 9SA
Tel 01904 646940
www.cliffordstower.com

York Minster

www.yorkminster.org

Merchant Adventurer's Hall

Fossgate, York, YO1 9XD
Tel: 01904 654818
www.theyorkcompany.co.uk

Treasurer's House NT

Minster Yard, York,
North Yorkshire, YO1 7JL
Tel: 01904 624247
www.nationaltrust.org.uk

National Railway Museum

Leeman Road, York, YO26 4XJ
Tel: 08448 153139
www.nrm.org.uk

Ripon Cathedral

www.riponcathedral.org.uk

Fountains Abbey

Ripon Nr Harrogate,
North Yorkshire, HG4 3DY
Tel: 01765 608888
www.nationaltrust.org.uk .

Markenfield Hall

Ripon, North Yorkshire, HG4 3AD
Tel: 01765 692 303
www.markenfield.com

East Riding

BEVERLEY AND HUMBERSIDE

Beverley Minster

Minster Yard North,
Beverley, HU17 0DP
Tel: 01482 868540
www.beverleyminster.org

St Mary's, Beverley

St Mary's Court, North Bar Within,
Beverley HU17 8DG
Tel: 01482 881437
www.stmarysbeverley.org.uk

Wilberforce House, Hull
23–25 High Street, Hull, HU1 1NQ
Tel: 01482 300300
www.hullcc.gov.uk

HOLY TRINITY CHURCH, HULL

Market Place,
Kingston upon Hull, HU1 1RR
Tel: 01482 324835
www.holy-trinity.org.uk

THE DEEP AQUARIUM, HULL

Tower Street, Hull,
North Humberside HU1 4DP
Tel: 01482 381000
www.thedeep.co.uk

FORT PAULL

Battery Road, Paull,
Hull, HU12 8FP
Tel: 01482 896236
www.fortpaull.com

HOLDERNESS
AND THE COAST

ST AUGUSTINE, HEDON

Tel: 01482 897693
www.staugustine-hedon.org.uk

ST PATRICK'S PATRINGTON

Northside, Patrington,
Hull, HU12 0PA
Tel: 01964 630327

ST GERMAIN, WINESTEAD

Winestead, East Yorkshire,
HU12 0NR
Tel: 01964 630327

BURTON CONSTABLE HALL

Skirlaugh, East Yorkshire, HU11 4LN
Tel: 01964 562400
www.burtonconstable.com

BRIDLINGTON PRIORY

Church Green, YO16 7JX
Tel: 01262 601938
www.bridlingtonpriory.co.uk

YORKSHIRE WOLDS

SLEDMERE HOUSE

Driffield, East Yorkshire, YO25 3XG
Tel: 01377 236637
www.sledmerehouse.com

BURTON AGNES HALL

Burton Agnes, East Yorkshire,
YO25 4NB
www.burtonagnes.com

WHARRAM PERCY

www.english-heritage.org.uk

VALE OF YORK
BURNBY HALL GARDENS

The Balk, Pocklington,
York, YO42 2QF
www.burnbyhallgardens.com

North Riding

HISTORIC CLEVELAND

TRANSPORTER BRIDGE, MIDDLESBROUGH

Ferry Road, Middlesbrough
Tel: 01642 247563 or 07624 819010

ORMESBY HALL NT

Church Lane, Ormesby,
  Redcar & Cleveland, TS7 9AS
  Tel: 01642 324188
  www.nationaltrust.org.uk

KIRKLEATHAM OLD HALL MUSEUM

Kirkleatham, Redcar, TS10 5NW
  Tel: 01642 479500

KIRKLEATHAM OWL CENTRE

Kirkleatham Village,
  Redcar, TS10 5NW
  Tel: 01642 480512
  www.kirkleathamowlcentre.org.uk

GUISBOROUGH PRIORY

Church Street,
  Guisborough, TS14 6HG
  Tel: 01287 633801

CAPTAIN COOK BIRTHPLACE MUSEUM

Stewart Park, Marton,
  Middlesbrough, TS7 8AT
  Tel 01642 311211
  www.captcook-ne.co.uk

CAPTAIN COOK & STAITHES HERITAGE CENTRE

High Street, Staithes, Nr Whitby,
  North Yorkshire, TS13 5BQ
  Tel: 01947 841454
  www.captaincookatstaithes.co.uk

CAPTAIN COOK MEMORIAL MUSEUM

Grape Lane, Whitby, YO22 4BA
  Tel: 01947 601900
  www.cookmuseumwhitby.co.uk

NORTH RIDING COAST

SCARBOROUGH CASTLE

Castle Road, Scarborough,
  YO11 1HY
  Tel: 01723 372451
  www.english-heritage.org.uk

THE ROTUNDA MUSEUM

Vernon Road, Scarborough
  Tel: 01723 353665
  www.rotundamuseum.co.uk

SIR GEORGE CAYLEY'S WORKSHOP

Brompton-by-Sawdon,
  Scarborough, YO13 9DJ

WHITBY ABBEY

Tel: 01947 603568
  www.english-heritage.co.uk

ST MARY'S CHURCH, WHITBY

Tel: 01947 602674
www.whitbyonline.co.uk

NORTH YORKSHIRE MOORS

RIEVAULX ABBEY

Rievaulx, N. Yorkshire, YO62 5LB
Tel: 01439 798228
www.english-heritage.co.uk

RIEVAULX TERRACES

Rievaulx, Helmsley,
North Yorkshire, YO62 5LJ
Tel: 01439 798340
www.nationaltrust.org.uk

DUNCOMBE PARK

Helmsley, York,
North Yorkshire, YO62 5EB
Tel: 01439 772625
or 01439 770213
www.duncombepark.com

HELMSLEY CASTLE

Tel: 01439 770442
www.english-heritage.co.uk

MOUNT GRACE PRIORY

Staddle Bridge, Northallerton,
North Yorkshire, DL6 3JG
Tel: 01609 883494
www.nationaltrust.org.uk

MOUSEMAN VISITOR CENTRE

Kilburn, York,
North Yorkshire, YO61 4AH
Tel: 01347 869100
or 01347 869102
www.robertthompsons.co.uk

NORTH YORKSHIRE MOORS RAILWAY

12 Park St, Pickering,
North Yorkshire, YO18 7AJ
Tel: 01751 472508
www.nymr.co.uk

NORTH RIDING DALES

BOLTON CASTLE

Nr Leyburn,
North Yorkshire, dl8 4et
Tel: 01969 623981
www.boltoncastle.co.uk

MIDDLEHAM CASTLE

Tel: 01969 623899
www.english-heritage.co.uk

RICHMOND CASTLE

Tel: 01748 822493
www.english-heritage.co.uk

EASBY ABBEY

Nr Richmond, N.Yorkshire
www.english-heritage.co.uk

NORTH RIDING HILLS AND VALES

THE WORLD OF JAMES HERRIOT

23 Kirkgate, Thirsk,
  North Yorkshire, YO7 1PL
  Tel: 01845 524234
  www.worldofjamesherriot.org

SHANDY HALL

Coxwold, N. Yorkshire, YO61 4AD
  Tel: 01347 868465
  www.shandean.org/shandyhall.html

NEWBURGH PRIORY

Newburgh, Coxwold, York,
  North Yorkshire, YO61 4AS
  Tel: 01347 868372
  www.newburghpriory.co.uk

CASTLE HOWARD

York, North Yorkshire, YO60 7DA
  Tel: 01653 648444
  www.castlehoward.co.uk

BYLAND ABBEY

Nr Coxwold, North Yorkshire,
  YO61 4BD
  Tel: 01347 868614
  www.english-heritage.co.uk

NUNNINGTON HALL

Nunnington, near York,
  North Yorkshire, YO62 5UY
  Tel: 01439 748283
  www.nationaltrust.org.uk

BENINGBROUGH HALL

Beningbrough, York,
  North Yorkshire, YO30 1DD
  Tel: 01904 472027
  www.nationaltrust.org.uk

West Riding

AIREDALE

National Media Museum
  Bradford, West Yorkshire, BD1 1NQ
  Tel: 08707 010200
  www.nationalmediamuseum.org.uk

BRADFORD CATHEDRAL

1 Stott Hill, Bradford, BD1 4EH
  Tel: 01274 777720
  www.bradfordcathedral.co.uk

BOLLING HALL

Bowling Hall Road,
  Bradford, BD4 7LP
  Tel: 01274 431814
  or 01274 431826
  www.bradfordmuseums.org/
  bollinghall/index.htm

SALTAIRE

Victoria Street, Saltaire, BD18 3LA
  www.saltairevillage.info

BRONTE PARSONAGE

Haworth, Keighley,
  West Yorkshire, BD22 8DR
  Tel: 01535 642323
  www.bronte.org.uk

KEIGHLEY AND WORTH VALLEY RAILWAY

Railway Station, Station Road,
  Haworth, Keighley, BD22 8NJ
  Tel: 01535 645214
  www.kwvr.co.uk

EAST RIDDLESDEN HALL

Bradford Road, Keighley,
  West Yorkshire, BD20 5EL
  Tel: 01535 607075
  www.nationaltrust.co.uk

KIRKSTALL ABBEY

12 Abbey Gorse, Leeds, LS5 3EH
  Tel: 0845 7654321
  www.leeds.gov.uk/kirkstallAbbey

MIDDLETON RAILWAY

The Station, Moor Road, Hunslet,
Leeds, West Yorkshire, LS10 2JQ
Tel: 01132 710320
www.middletonrailway.org.uk

SHIPLEY GLEN CABLE TRAMWAY

Prod Lane, Baildon, Shipley,
West Yorkshire, BD17 5BN
Tel: 01274 589010
www.glentramway.co.uk

CLIFFE CASTLE MUSEUM, KEIGHLEY

Spring Gardens Lane, Keighley,
West Yorkshire, BD20 6LH
Tel: 01535 618231
www.bradfordmuseums.org/cliffecastle

TEMPLE NEWSAM

Temple Newsam Road, off Selby
Road,
Leeds, LS15 0AE
Tel: 01132 645535
www.leeds.gov.uk/templenewsam

DON VALLEY

ABBEYDALE HAMLET

Abbeydale Road South,
Sheffield, S7 2QW
Tel: 01142 367731
www.simt.co.uk

TURRET HOUSE

115 Manor Lane, Sheffield, S2 1UH
Tel: 01142 762828

CONISBROUGH CASTLE

Castle Hill, Conisbrough,
Doncaster,
South Yorkshire, DN12 3BU
Tel: 01709 863329
www.conisbroughcastle.org.uk

KIRKLEES AND CALDER VALLEY

WAKEFIELD CATHEDRAL

Wakefield, WF1 1PJ
Tel: 01924 373923
www.wakefieldcathedral.org.uk

NOSTELL PRIORY

Doncaster Road, Nostell, near
Wakefield,
West Yorkshire, WF4 1QE
Tel: 01924 863892
www.nationaltrust.org.uk

PONTEFRACT CASTLE

Castle Lodge, Castle Chain,
Pontefract, WF8 1QH
Tel: 01924 302703

WAINHOUSE TOWER, HALIFAX

Open some weekends

SHIBDEN HALL

Lister's Road, Halifax, HX3 6XG
Tel: 01422 352246
or 01422 321455
www.calderdale.gov.uk

VICTORIA TOWER

Off Lumb Lane, Almondbury,
Huddersfield, HD4 6TA
www.kirklees.gov.uk

WEST RIDING DALES AND THE OUSE

*The postal address for these attrac-
tions is North Yorkshire but they
are in the West Riding.

SKIPTON CASTLE

Skipton, North Yorkshire, BD23 1AW
Tel: 01756 792442
www.skiptoncastle.co.uk

MOTHER SHIPTON'S CAVE

Prophecy Lodge, High Bridge,
Knaresborough, North Yorkshire,
HG5 8DD
Tel: 01423 864600
www.mothershiptonscave.com

SELBY ABBEY

The Crescent, Selby, YO8 4PU
Tel: 01757 703123
www.selbyabbey.org.uk

WHITE SCAR CAVE

Ingleton, North Yorkshire, LA6 3AW
Tel: 01524 241244
www.whitescarcave.co.uk

Index of People

Index of Places

Acknowledgements

Mai and I would like to thank Susan Davey and Martin Vander Weyer for letting us stay in their beautiful homes while we were touring Yorkshire. And many thanks also to the Marquess of Zetland, Sir Richard and Lady Storey, and Philip and Sally Bean for their hospitality, and to Mark and Belinda Evans for giving us the opportunity to see Sir George Cayley's workshop, a highlight of our trip.

Special thanks as always from me to the marvellous team at Ebury: Publishing Director Carey Smith for her unstinting support and encouragement; Senior Editor Imogen Fortes for her patience and wise advice; the wonderful teams at sales and publicity; and editor Steve Dobell.

Thanks, too, to my agent Ros.

Mai, your talent grows with every book and your beauty with every day. Thank you.